TRAVELING SOULS

TRAVELING SOULS

Contemporary Pilgrimage Stories

edited by
BRIAN BOULDREY

foreword by
PICO IYER

WHEREABOUTS PRESS
San Francisco

Published in the United States by
Whereabouts Press
PMB 703
3145 Geary Boulevard
San Francisco, California 94118
www.whereaboutspress.com

Distributed to the trade by
Consortium Book Sales & Distribution

Manufactured in the United States of America.

Library of Congress Cataloging-in-Publication Data

Traveling souls : contemporary pilgrimage stories /
edited Brian Bouldrey;
foreword by Pico Iyer
p.   cm.
ISBN 1-883513-08-1 (alk. paper)
1. Voyages and travels.
2. Travelers' writings.
3. Pilgrims and pilgrimages.
I. Bouldrey, Brian.
G525.T664 1999
910.4—dc21   99-051345

5   4   3   2   1

CONTENTS

A JOURNEY INTO CANDLELIGHT

Every journey is a question of sorts, and the best journeys for me are the ones in which every answer opens onto deeper and more searching questions. Every traveler is on a quest of sorts, but the pilgrim stands out because his every step is a leap of faith, and his journey is through such states as penitence and prayer. Unlike a typical adventurer, the pilgrim seeks not to conquer the worlds he visits but to surrender to them; and unlike a missionary, he seeks not to preach but, in the silence of his supplication, to listen. A pilgrim does not have to be moving toward something holy, I think, so much as toward whatever resides in the deepest part of him: it could be a poet who gave wings to his soul, or a lover who broke his heart open. The most eternal pilgrim in literature—always referred to as such—is Romeo.

Yet even as the pilgrim thinks she knows where, and why, she's going, the beauty of every trip is that circumstances are far wiser than she is, and she seldom ends up where she expected to. Her unseen partner on the road is serendipity. Several years ago, too settled in an office in Rockefeller Center in New York, I decided to travel to the land I'd always dreamed of,

Japan; I wanted to learn about simplicity and kindness in a monastery. I flew over to Kyoto, checked into a Zen temple on the backstreets, and, after a week or so, found that the routine was much more familiar than I'd expected. So I stepped out, and instantly found much of the compassion and wisdom I'd been seeking—in the modern city all around, the woman standing at the temple gates. God comes to see us, as Emerson writes, without bell.

Like anyone, I've taken my pilgrimages in every direction of my inner compass, and to every corner of the shrine I carry round inside me. Our souls are always traveling, of course, and whatever we find in Jerusalem we could also find at home. Yet the very fact of moving quickens our attention, and jettisons our habits, in a way that leaves us wide awake to what otherwise we might take for granted. So I have gone to Taos, to see where D. H. Lawrence conducted his "savage pilgrimage"; to Tibet, where local pilgrims walk for months on end, across the empty plains, prostrating themselves every step of the way; to Cambodia, most recently to see how people live amid ghosts and broken memories. Once, traveling to the rock caves around Lalibela, in Ethiopia, by mule, through a landscape of cedar trees and olives, I was humbled to notice that the people all around me had come on foot, traveling for weeks in dusty robes, while fasting. Why had they come to this unprepossessing spot? Because, they said, between joyful ululations, to come here was to come to heaven.

In the mind's eye, a pilgrimage is generally a straight line, from here to there (from being lost to being found); in practice, however, it is more often a kind of circle, as in the ritual circumambulations that worshipers make in Tibet, in India, or around the Islamic Ka'ba. A pilgrim's journey, unlike a traveler's, never ends; it only deepens. That is the thrust of Bunyan's *Pilgrim's Progress*—that all our life is a pilgrimage—and it is part of the reason, I'm sure, why so many religions have a tradition of mendicancy and wandering. The great contemporary pilgrims—I'm thinking here of Annie Dillard and Peter Brook, Van Morrison and John le Carré (a "secret pilgrim," like many of us)—are all essentially traveling deeper into faith and doubt at the same time: deeper into complexity. In that sense, it matters little whether they're surrounded by tolling bells or clanging sirens.

Yet reading the wonderfully varied and unexpected stories assembled here, I was struck by how much the notion of pilgrimage today has to do with retrieving a sense of purpose (and simplicity, and constancy); with putting oneself, quite literally, in the footsteps of the past. Once upon a less secular time, almost everyone made pilgrimages, and most of the great works of our early literature—Dante's ascent into the stars, Chaucer's wanderers to Canterbury, the tales of Orpheus and Odysseus and Hercules—commemorate both inward and outward journeys; these days, I suspect, many of us travel in part to experience pilgrimage by proxy. Most of the travelers in this volume leave home, as I have done, to partake of someone else's pilgrimage, and so to learn what animates people to undertake such sacrificial tasks; the destination of pilgrimage is pilgrimage itself.

It's striking, too, to see how many of these travelers are moving deliberately backward. They go on foot—a relative luxury in a time of cars and trains and planes—and they travel, often, in simple, anonymous robes, with a staff, petitioning, as monks do, for their food and shelter. In an age of flashing screens and jumbo jets, the pilgrim is a traveler into candlelight. And a large part of the discipline he embraces comes in the sloughing off of self—literally (as when Michael Wolfe becomes just another hajji, generally addressed as Roy Thomas) and metaphorically (as in Barbara Wilson's searing account of how pain and rage in the desert annulled her previous stories of herself). "Abandon self, all ye who enter here" could be the inscription written on the pilgrim's door; Rachel Kadish's powerful memoir reminds us that we travel partially to return to selves we have forgotten, or people we didn't know we were (for worse as much as better).

Of course the pilgrim, like any traveler, is mostly traveling inside herself, to a destination not found on any map. Yet there is a palpable benefit in making the trip physically, on foot: the very feel of stones in Jerusalem,

Alane Salierno Mason says, "has a charismatic effect on the whole body," much as, perhaps, the very act of getting down on our knees releases in us a kind of humanity and sweetness. The wonder, the intensity, the electricity of pilgrimage are infectious—passed on like a holy fever—and in Michael Wolfe's ecstatic account of making the trip to Makkah, we can feel the fires burning in every pilgrim's heart (if Wolfe had stayed in California, he'd have thought his destination was "Mecca").

Distinctions get buried on the road, and the pilgrim is keeping company with kindred spirits from distant centuries and continents; the first pilgrim to Canterbury, we learn here, walking on his knees, was a king, Henry II, traveling to atone for his execution of Thomas à Becket. Even here in my neighborhood in Japan, when I travel to my local temple I am taken out of the age I know, often, by the sight of *yamabushi,* or mountain pilgrims, done up in an outlandish shamanic gear of trinkets and cowrie shells and deer skins. The pilgrim moves into a realm of talismans and spells.

In a sense, these powerful souls remind us, all pilgrimage is a trial, and its adherents are tested by the road; the pilgrim is like the hero in some classic fairy tale, asked to perform various deeds of heroism and cunning to prove his love. Except in this case, the person asking is himself. In Japan, when he was growing up, a ninety-year-old Zen painter once told me, children were taught to pay for suffering (it is such a privilege, and a catalyst for growth); in our more comfortable cultures, many people have to go abroad, on pilgrimage, to measure themselves against a pain that is reality. The heart of all our faiths is *religio,* or a rebinding, as the Latin term suggests.

The final thing that hits me, traveling with these contemporary pilgrims, is how fluid and beyond boundaries our pilgrims are today, in a world that's stepping across borders every minute: Gretel Ehrlich, a modern American, treads a Buddhist path in China, just as many Chinese make similar trips of worship to the Holy Land that is America (founded, after all, by pilgrims, and "discovered" by another votary who thought he'd come to India). A Christian learns from Buddhist monks, and agnostics learn from Christians. I, though born a Hindu, have never been to the Hindu holy place of Varanasi—and yet have been lucky enough, in our mobile world, to sit before Notre Dame and Ayers Rock and the Buddhist caves of Laos. "To study the Way is to study the self," the great Zen teacher Dogen said. "To study the self is to forget the self. To forget the self is to be enlightened by all things. To be thus enlightened is to remove the barriers between one's self and others."

At the end of every pilgrimage, of course, you learn that ends are new beginnings, and that you see only what you brought with you (besides, "If you can understand it," as Augustine says, "then it is not God"). The main point of climbing to an icy cave in India, where a sadhu sits, is to realize (as Anne Cushman says) that one might be better off in California; except if one had remained in California, one would have always had unanswered questions about an icy cave in India. In any case, whatever is discovered cannot—or need not—be spelled out. "It is in *seeking* truth that we find enlightenment," the Catholic Father Laurence Freeman writes, "not in declaring it."

Thus the final redeeming beauty of the pilgrimage is that no step on such a trip is wasted, and whatever happens, however difficult, is good. "To seek God is to find him," said Gregory of Nyssa, "to find God is to seek him." Peter Matthiessen travels to Nepal to find the snow leopard and discovers that the main lesson he must learn comes from not finding the animal; Graham Greene goes to Mexico during the time of the persecution of priests and finds his modern savior in a broken, squalid "whisky priest," who forgets himself by reaching out toward the suffering.

And so we go on taking pilgrimages, in part because every discovery, however unlooked-for, is a step forward; but also, more deeply, because every one of us carries around, inside, a certain, unnamed homesickness, a longing for a place we left and don't know how to find again (the vision seen by Meaulnes in the haunting Alain-Fournier novel, the vanished

Shangri-La sought by Conway in *Lost Horizon*). If there is a Golden Age behind us, we believe, there may be one ahead of us too. A pilgrim, ultimately, is a traveler moving toward the light, a light she hopes to collect and scatter across her path; where an adventurer may seek out a distant planet, the pilgrim only seeks the sun.

"All the way to heaven," as Catherine of Siena writes, "is heaven."

Pico Iyer

NARA, JAPAN, JUNE 1999

PREFACE

The gathering of these personal essays has coincided with a boom in pilgrimages and memoirs about pilgrimage. Great minds think alike—the ink was still drying on the agreements for this collection when the pope announced special dispensations to Catholics who elected to make a pilgrimage in the millennium years.

The world's sacred and ancient pilgrimage sites—Varanasi, Rome, Jerusalem, Mecca, Santiago—are receiving huge numbers of pilgrims. Meanwhile, in America, a relatively young country, we have begun to assemble our own set of sacred sites. Some of them have a less sacred quality, such as Graceland, Iowa's Field of Dreams, and Disneyland. But this collection, in which Alice Walker makes her way to the birthplace of Zora Neale Hurston or John Hanson Mitchell walks where Thoreau walked, suggests that American pilgrimage sites are more personal, less popular in the purest sense of that word. Even so, every day more people participate in epic walk- and bike-a-thons for charity, and in some ways, these strenuous solo acts could be seen as the all-American way of seeking out the contemplative life. The existence of so many forms of pilgrimage made it difficult to define it for the purposes of *Traveling Souls*—for who am I to decide what is and isn't a pilgrimage? While Joshua Tree isn't on the pope's list of holy destinations, the story Barbara Wilson tells about her journey through that landscape has everything to do with what pilgrimage is about.

Why, besides the millennium, are so many of us going on pilgrimage? In 1996, I, spindly legged, uncoordinated, and lacking a sense of direction, strapped on a pack and walked through southern France and across northern Spain to the cathedral of Santiago de Compostela, a journey marvelously described here by Abigail Seymour (and based on my own personal prejudice, therefore, her story opens this collection). In my journal, I compiled a list of the reasons I was walking: art, architecture, history, spirituality, exercise, to escape the twentieth century—and most of all, *to be alone.*

I tried to be alone, I really did. But along the way, I met a rogue's gallery of fellow pilgrims, a gang to rival Chaucer's merry band. I recall a day very early in my pilgrimage, when I met an old, fit man who was spending his retirement maintaining a bit of trail in Basque France. For a stretch, he walked alongside me—wouldn't leave my side, in fact, as he exhorted me to spend the pilgrimage solo. He said it would be good for my soul, my heart, my body, my mind. It seemed urgent to him—as if he thought it was something that was difficult to achieve, this aloneness. That it would be so difficult was hard for me to imagine there in the middle of the Pyrenees, on my own.

But the old man knew. The closer you are to the beginning of a pilgrim road, the emptier it is. But later, pilgrims funnel in from other roads until, as you near your goal, the trail becomes a party. And then you are not alone.

To be alone. In our age of package tours and multiplying travel magazines, pilgrims are independent types who desire some journey off the beaten path, something original, something meaningful. And yet pilgrimage is the ultimate package tour—in many cases people have taken the same road for thousands of years. Pilgrims seldom do the road alone.

Nor did I: despite all my intentions to walk alone and contemplate life, I fell in with philandering British sea captains, snoring Swiss schoolteachers, Spanish bullfighters, reluctant Dutch retirees, Belgian prisoners, engineers, scholars, wonks, admen, New Age fakes, doctors, students. The pilgrim road is rowdy.

And perhaps that is exactly what American pilgrims want. We've been so successful at insulating ourselves by living in our cul-de-sac developments and airtight autos and anonymous high-rises that we have cut ourselves off from all the wonderful strangers and surprises of the world.

In these essays, you will encounter, along with pilgrim authors, strangers and surprises to no end—Satish Kumar can't convince strangers that he prefers to walk as he tramps through England; Rachel Kadish tries to make strangers her family in a journey to Poland; Malcolm X estranges himself—for the Malcolm X who left for Mecca was not the same Malcolm X who returned.

I am reminded of an extraordinary pilgrim I met on the way to Santiago. He was a gypsy, a cross-eyed gypsy. He was on the road to Santiago but traveling backward, heading, he told me, to Rome. He was swimming against the tide of westward-walking pilgrims. In a small bar near the French border, he drank coffee with me and I taught him how to say "Do you have any money for a poor pilgrim?" in French. In return, he gave me his ratty little list of hostels I would encounter along the road, places he'd already been. He had categorized the refuges as either good or bad, and, I learned later, he was right every time. I had just entered Spain and didn't have the money to pay for my coffee, so he paid for mine. A gypsy, walking backward, who did nothing but give. He was totally alone, getting more alone every day. No pilgrim deserved a comrade more.

You too will begin this book alone, curled up with a handful of strangers in the most exotic locales: Alane Salierno Mason navigates you through Jerusalem, the spiritual city of three major religions; Anne Cushman seeks a sadhu in remote India. Their reasons for going are varied. Jennifer Lash, fighting cancer, seeks consolation at Lourdes, and Marvin Barrett seeks a second chance after his own illness; Michael Wolfe travels to Mecca as a converted Muslim; Gretel Ehrlich is an American Buddhist in China. All of these writers approach the assay of a pilgrimage with the wonder and adventure that's necessary. They begin the journey alone, but they don't finish that way. Neither will you.

For me, assembling this book has been another kind of pilgrimage, one full of surprises, encounters with strangers, and very little time to be alone. I could identify fellow pilgrims in a flash and dismiss pretenders just as quickly. And yet, for all the recognition, there are also strangers here. Even the accounts of my now-familiar Santiago have an element of foreignness to them, because Seymour's experiences were entirely different from mine. Every person might take that same pilgrimage and bring home another story. And that is why pilgrimage is at once the ultimate package tourist deal and the most original, adventurous kind of travel.

I would like to thank Dave Peattie and Ellen Towell, the masterminds at Whereabouts Press, who worked closely with me, guiding me, keeping me on track, helping me find the pieces of the puzzle, and keeping their cool. I also want to thank Michael Lowenthal, James Morrison, Abigail Seymour, Bob Gluck, Miriam Wolf, and Mary Capello.

Let this collection be your inspiration to take your own pilgrimage.

ULTREYA

A man sleeping on the cot next to mine was snoring. He had a kerchief over his face that flapped each time he let out a breath. It was 2:30 in the morning. The other fifty or so people in the musty room of the monastery were sound asleep. I felt pale and soft and timid, among people who seemed to sleep the sound sleep of certainty.

Roncesvalles, the monastery where we were staying in the Pyrenees, is the gateway into Spain from France on the Camino de Santiago. It was my first night on the pilgrimage; I was the only American and one of the few women in the group, as far as I could tell. Most of the people were traveling in groups of three or four, and some were in couples. I was alone.

Sleepless, I walked down the three flights of wooden stairs, worn in a rut down the middle. They led me to a stone entryway, the spot that in a few hours would be the start of my walk to Santiago de Compostela, five hundred miles away. There was a ring around the moon. The road faded into a gray, gauzy haze.

"Lord, hear my prayer."

The sound of my own voice, hollow and thin, startled me. I had long ago given up the idea that anyone or anything could hear me. Feeling chilled, I went back inside.

When I awoke the next morning, most of the beds were empty. My fellow pilgrims had already set out before 5:00, before it was even light. I left two and a half hours later than they did and had the path to myself, sure that I had beaten the system. But by noon I was caught in the blazing sun, four more miles away from the next refuge. As I clumped down the mountain, trying to gauge how much my legs hurt, I came upon Burguete, a tiny whitewashed town where Hemingway stayed during the bullfight season. No sign of any fiestas, just windows shuttered against the heat and a lone bar open.

Just outside of town was a series of wooden signs with only one word: *¡Ultreya!* My guidebook told me that it was a cognate of the Latin *ulter,* the same root as the English *ultra.* It was the ancient greeting exchanged by medieval pilgrims. "Beyond!" they cried to one another. "Go beyond!" Their destination, and mine, was the cathedral in Santiago de Compostela, Spain. Inside is a marble pillar carved into a Jesse Tree, the depiction of the prophecy of Jesus' birth from the book of Isaiah: "A shoot shall come from the stump of Jesse, and a branch shall grow out of its roots." The marble tree's trunk bears an indentation in the shape of a human hand that has been worn over a millennium by millions of pilgrims. Legend says that if you put your right hand against the pillar and touch your forehead three times to the statue just below it, you will be blessed.

This act of faith is the culmination of a five hundred–mile walk from the Spanish border with France to the spot where the remains of Apostle James were said to have been unearthed. The story goes that Saint James was beheaded in Jerusalem and his body was carried in a divinely guided boat to the western coast of Spain, where he lay undiscovered for 750 years. One night, an old hermit named Pelayo saw a series of bright lights floating in the sky above a field. He began digging on the spot and discovered a well-preserved body and a note identifying the remains as Santiago—Saint James himself.

Soon after Pelayo's revelation, people began walking across Europe to venerate Saint James. At the height of the shrine's popularity in the eleventh century, more than half a million people a year walked to Santiago de Compostela. The route, which crosses the Pyrenees, Navarre, and the plains of Castile and ends in the lush hills of Galicia, became an important trade road. Merchants set up shop to cater to the crowds of people pouring in, and churches and monasteries were erected to house them. "Santiago," wrote the German philosopher Goethe, "built Europe."

The pilgrimage never died out; in fact, its popularity has surged since the Camino was named a UNESCO World Heritage Site in 1985. It remains largely unchanged since the Middle Ages, with the exception of a long, ugly stretch along a busy highway in the middle of the country. Friends of the Camino associations across Spain are working hard to divert the footpath in a safer direction without losing any of its authenticity. Pilgrim refuges have been built for modern-day seekers, providing bunk beds, cold showers, and kitchens, all staffed by former-pilgrim volunteers. During the Holy Year in 1993 (when the Feast of St. James, July 25, fell on a Sunday), one hundred thousand people walked, bicycled, or rode on horseback the length of the Camino.

I never thought I would be one of them. I am not Spanish. I was raised a Protestant. And I am not hardy by nature. I was the sort of timid child who kept her white Keds on throughout the summer for fear of stepping on a bee. I honestly can't say for what or for whom I decided to walk to Santiago myself.

All I know is that I did walk there, all the way, and that it changed me.

I was twenty-eight years old and had just gone through a divorce. I had left Manhattan with the notion of shedding my possessions and disappearing overseas. Maybe I could create myself anew, I thought, become someone more varied and textured. I came to Europe with a list of all the cities I planned to visit: Paris, Moscow, Munich, Prague, Barcelona, Athens—I never wanted to stop moving. I got a job in Madrid teaching English to businesspeople and lived in a small apartment in the center of the city.

I spent my first Spanish Thanksgiving dinner sitting across the table from a clean-cut young American student in a bow tie. He was thin and eager and soft around the edges. I forgot his name before the end of the evening, and then I forgot about him entirely.

Meanwhile, a creeping loneliness had tracked me down again, making me feel that was time to start moving. But I didn't know where to go.

Six months later I was introduced at a party to an earthy, handsome man in faded jeans and sandals. He had long hair, an earring, and a scallop-shell pendant around his neck. It took me a few minutes to recognize him without his bow tie—it was my Thanksgiving dinner companion, utterly transformed.

"I have walked across Spain," Jamie told me, "along the Camino de Santiago."

In those words I found what I had been looking for—whatever had changed him could change me, too.

So I set out that August for the monastery of Roncesvalles. The Camino appealed to me because I would never have to stop moving—I even thought I might stay on it forever, live on it, walking back and forth, becoming one of its eccentric fixtures, another character people would meet along the way. That was how I ended up sleepless that first night among strangers near the border of France, ready to walk through the wilderness—Spain's and my own.

The Camino is as varied as the people who travel it. It is moody and changeable, sometimes a dripping forest path of overhanging trees with not a soul in sight, other times an exhaust-filled highway with semis whizzing by and crowds of people clogging the way. It has bridges and hills and rivers—things to cross and climb and navigate.

After about a week of walking alone, I fell in with a group of people who, although we never actually declared our allegiance, remained more or less together for the rest of the trip. There were about twenty of us disbanding and reforming each night and morning. They included Manuel, a big, lumbering, mustachioed man who worked as a cobbler in Valencia and laughed so hard at his own jokes that he would have to stop walking. He warned us that sometimes he talked and sang in his sleep, and, indeed, a few nights later he sat bolt upright shouting, "Chickens for sale! Chickens for sale!"

His constant companion was Sergio, a quiet vending-machine sales-man from the south of Spain, who revealed one night after dinner that he had learned he had cancer two years before, at the age of thirty-two. When his cancer went into remission, Sergio made a vow to walk the Camino in thanksgiving—and there he was. *"A Santiago nunca se llega, solo se va,"* he said. "You never get to Santiago, you only set out for it."

Then there was Geert, a Dutch bus driver with no front teeth, who en-joyed a breakfast each morning of two yogurts and a Heineken. Another fellow traveler, Christine, was a doctoral candidate from Switzerland who wrote in her journal every night by flashlight.

We compared blisters and bandaged joints, pored over one another's maps, and listened wide-eyed to Camino veterans tell of what lay in store for us. We were advised to ask for Pablo in a village up ahead. The old man, they said, would give us each a perfectly whittled walking stick. We heard about Tomás, a self-proclaimed Knight of the Templar who lived in the mountains, carrying on his defunct monastic order's tradition of pro-tecting the pilgrims. We were told of a fountain that spouted wine instead of water, and about a stained-glass window, made of every color in the rainbow, where the light nonetheless shone through white instead of tinted. We were urged to stop at Molinaseca, a town so inviting that swim-ming-pool ladders were installed on its riverbanks. I was given a scallop shell, the traditional symbol of the Camino, to wear around my neck. Its magical properties would protect me from evil.

I happened to be walking alone on the fourth day when I entered the little village of Zariquiegui, near Pamplona. Every window and door was shuttered against the midafternoon heat, but three backpacks were propped against the wall of the village church. I peered inside toward the darkened nave. All was quiet. Light angled down through a window near the ceiling in dusty rays, and I stood with the cool wood of the door against my back as it closed. It was completely quiet—and then I heard someone take a breath. Out of the darkness near the altar came three voices singing in a cappella harmony. The hair stood up on the back of my sweaty arms. I crept into the last pew and listened. As my eyes came into focus I saw that the singers were fellow pilgrims: two men and a woman in their twenties, wearing hiking boots, T-shirts, and shells around their necks. When they finished, I followed them back outside. They were German students who were walking to Santiago in segments, one week each year. They stopped in at every unlocked church along the way to sing.

"Why do you sing when no one else will hear you?" I asked.

"God can hear us," the woman said.

I found Pablo the whittler in the village of Ázqueta. He shyly handed me a walking stick, for which he refused to take any money. The river in Molinaseca also lived up to its reputation—the water was cool and sweet, and I lingered there during the hottest part of the afternoon. In the little town of Irache I actually found the fountain of wine. It turned out to be a marketing ploy set up by a local vintner, who had hooked up a tap to barrels of his house red. I never did find the miraculous stained glass window.

In the tenth-century village of Manjarín I met Tomás the Templar. He was the only dweller left in that ghost town, living in a chaotic camp in an old, partly roofed stone house. Tomás blessed me with a steel sword on both shoulders: *"El Camino es un rio,"* he said. "The Camino is a river— just ride it."

I found it easier to ride as I went. Even my nationality started to fade from me, like something left in the sun too long. I got browner, and my Spanish improved. If anything, people guessed I was British or German— never American, never me.

I walked for a total of twenty-eight days, from one full moon to the next, starting out with a backpack full of prissy toiletries, trendy halter tops, Band-Aids, and traveler's checks. By the time I wriggled out of my dinged-up pack for the last time, I had pared down to one change of clothes and a toothbrush.

On the last day I reached the hilltop of Monte de Gozo, where pilgrims used to dance and weep and hold each other at the first glimpse of the cathedral spires. It is now a touristy park with a view of the football stadium, a superhighway, and a rest stop. I had to ask someone to point out the spires, and even then I could barely make out three gray needles above the skyline. I wended my way through the old part of the city, still following the crude yellow arrows that had guided me that far. Suddenly, I rounded a corner and there it was. I looked up at the spires and the sun shone right into my eyes. I continued on through an archway and into the grand plaza that faces the astonishing, ornate facade.

Inside the cathedral, the marble Jesse Tree supports an entire carved entryway. In the middle of this tall "Doorway of Glory," Santiago is seated peacefully. As I waited in line, leaning on the walking stick that Pablo had made me, it became clear that everyone up ahead was following exactly the same ritual, although slightly different from the version I was prepared for: they touched the pillar, reached into a stone lion's mouth to the right, and then bent to tap their forehead three times. When my turn came I did the same thing. Eyes closed, lion's mouth, forehead, tap, tap, tap.

I looked up and noticed a uniformed guard standing nearby, his eyes at a bored half-mast, arms folded across his chest. "Excuse me," I said. "What is the significance of the lion's mouth?"

He shrugged. "Nothing. Some kid reached in there this morning and everybody who came after him's been doing it ever since."

And, for all I know, they still are. I like to think so, to imagine that I was another tiny thread in this rich fabric of tradition. Are the threads mere gossamer of fact? Skeptics will tell you that the scallop shell that protected me en route was the membership badge of an ancient Venus cult. Its members dwelt in the Celtic forests and practiced rituals that Christians would find shocking. Some scholars say that the divine revelation of the tomb's location was mistranscribed by a monk with poor eyesight. They say he probably looked at an early account of St. James's burial site whose Latin script said Hierosolyma (Jerusalem) and mistakenly wrote Hispania (Spain).

There are those who try to explain away the hermit Pelayo's vision, pointing to current astronomical phenomena. I doubt that any of them have been pilgrims. On the Camino there is a much finer line between an astronomical phenomenon and a miracle.

If I was expecting something miraculous in myself, though, it had yet to happen. I didn't feel anything except tired, and sad that it was over. I said good-bye to Manuel, Sergio, Christine, Geert, and the singing Germans, and I returned to Madrid.

I spent several weeks going over my snapshots and watching the blisters on my feet heal and disappear. My walking stick rested in the corner of the living room. I rode the subway and taught grammar classes and wrote, but I felt as though I had been separated from a loved one. I thought about the Camino all year, wondering what winter was like in the mountains of León and how they might celebrate Easter in Santiago. You might say I was homesick, if a journey can be a home.

So when it got warm again, I went back. I worked as a volunteer at one of the Camino refuges. I cleaned toilets and kept house for more than one thousand people in two weeks. I was restless and wanted to be among them. The day before I planned to begin my second pilgrimage, I started to feel strange. I was prickly with fevered goose bumps, and everything seemed too bright and too loud. I set out at dawn with a ringing in my right ear. By nightfall that ear was completely deaf. I was losing sensation in my cheek and temple, but I kept walking. León, Astorga, Ponferrada, Triacastela, mile after mile. "Beyond," I told myself. "Go beyond."

I kept walking until I couldn't stand the pain and pressure in my head. My hearing was shot, and I was angry that the one thing that had ever brought me peace—the Camino—was the very thing that was hurting me now.

Eight days away from Santiago I boarded a bus for Madrid. The doctor there told me that it was a good thing I'd come to him, since I was about eight days away from being dead—a staph infection I'd caught back at the refuge had been spreading through my ear on its way to my brain and spinal cord.

Although grateful to be alive, I still felt that I had failed. When I called my Camino-mates to tell them I hadn't made it the second time, Sergio just laughed: "Don't you remember? *A Santiago nunca se llega.*"

I thought about what he said as I tried to stitch my life back together and recover from the trip. My loss of hearing took on new meaning for me—I had always thought that nothing or no one could hear me; maybe I was the one not listening. I sat in a rocking chair near the window in my apartment on Calle Huertas and finally understood the obvious: "beyond" isn't about distance or the capacity to endure. And so I left the Camino permanently and began an altogether different journey, the search for a real home. After three years in Spain, I accepted a job offer in the United States, where I am living now.

My hearing is fully restored, and I try to be more open to what I hear. I have gone beyond. I like to remember my last night in Santiago after I finished the Camino. I was lying on my back in the middle of the deserted Plaza Obradoiro, gazing up at the cathedral. Suddenly I heard someone chattering at me from the far side of the plaza. I couldn't quite hear what she was saying, but I assumed it was along the lines of "Get up off the street, young lady!" Instead, the woman came over and sat beside me, then spun around and gestured for me to do the same.

"*¡Al revés! ¡Al revés!*" she commanded. "Turn around—the view is much better the other way."

The two of us lay down side by side and looked at the cathedral upside down. She was right: the spires of Santiago no longer looked rooted to the earth, but seemed to rise up out of the sky.

MECCA

C AIRO AIRPORT, APRIL 1964 The literal meaning of *Hajj* in Arabic is to set out toward a definite objective. In Islamic law, it means to set out for the Ka'ba, the Sacred House, and to fulfill the pilgrimage rites. The Cairo airport was where scores of Hajj groups were becoming *muhrim*, pilgrims, upon entering the state of *ihram*, the assumption of a spiritual and physical state of consecration. Upon advice, I arranged to leave in Cairo all of my luggage and four cameras, one a movie camera. I had bought in Cairo a small valise, just big enough to carry one suit, shirt, a pair of underwear sets, and a pair of shoes into Arabia. Driving to the airport with our Hajj group, I began to get nervous, knowing that from there in, it was going to be watching others who knew what they were doing, and trying to do what they did.

Entering the state of *ihram*, we took off our clothes and put on two white towels. One, the *izar*, was folded around the loins. The other, the *rida*, was thrown over the neck and shoulders, leaving the right shoulder and arm bare. A pair of simple sandals, the *na'z* left the anklebones bare.

Over the *izar* waistwrapper, a money belt was worn, and a bag, something like a woman's big handbag, with a long strap, was for carrying the passport and other valuable papers, such as the letter I had from Dr. Shawarbi.

Every one of the thousands at the airport, about to leave for Jidda, was dressed this way. You could be a king or a peasant, and no one would know. Some powerful personages, who were discreetly pointed out to me, had on the same thing I had on. Once thus dressed, we all had begun intermittently calling out *"Labayk! Labayk!"* "Here I come, O Lord!" The airport sounded with the din of *muhrim* expressing their intention to perform the journey of the Hajj.

Planeloads of pilgrims were taking off every few minutes, but the airport was jammed with more, and their friends and relatives waiting to see them off. Those not going were asking others to pray for them at Mecca. We were on our plane, in the air, when I learned for the first time that with the crush, there was not supposed to have been space for me, but strings had been pulled, and someone had been put off because they didn't want to disappoint an American Muslim. I felt mingled emotions of regret that I had inconvenienced and discomfited whoever was bumped off the plane for me and, with that, an utter humility and gratefulness that I had been paid such an honor and respect.

Packed in the plane were white, black, brown, red, and yellow people, blue eyes and blond hair, and my kinky red hair—all together, brothers! All honoring the same God Allah, all in turn giving equal honor to each other.

From some in our group, the word was spreading from seat to seat that I was a Muslim from America. Faces turned, smiling toward me in greeting. A box lunch was passed out, and as we ate that, the word that a Muslim from America was aboard got up into the cockpit.

The captain of the plane came back to meet me. He was an Egyptian; his complexion was darker than mine; he could have walked in Harlem, and no one would have given him a second glance. He was delighted to meet an American Muslim. When he invited me to visit the cockpit, I jumped at the chance. . . .

JIDDA The Jidda airport seemed even more crowded than Cairo's had been. Our party became another shuffling unit in the shifting mass with every race on Earth represented. Each party was making its way toward the long line waiting to go through customs. Before reaching customs, each Hajj party was assigned a *mutawwif*, who would be responsible for transferring that party from Jidda to Mecca. Some pilgrims cried, "*Labayk!*" Others, sometimes large groups, were chanting in unison a prayer that I will translate: "I submit to no one but thee, O Allah. I submit to no one but thee. I submit to thee because thou hast no partner. All praise and blessings come from thee, and thou art alone in thy kingdom." The essence of the prayer is the oneness of God.

Only officials were not wearing the *ihram* garb, or the white skullcaps, long, white, nightshirt-looking gown, and the little slippers of the *mutawwif*, those who guided each pilgrim party, and their helpers. In Arabic, an *mmmm* sound before a verb makes a verbal noun, so *mutawwif* meant "the one who guides" the pilgrims on the *tawaf*, which is the circumambulation of the Ka'ba in Mecca.

I was nervous, shuffling in the center of our group in the line waiting to have our passports inspected. I had an apprehensive feeling. Look what I'm handing them. I'm in the Muslim world, right at the fountain. I'm handing them the American passport which signifies the exact opposite of what Islam stands for.

The judge in our group sensed my strain. He patted my shoulder. Love, humility, and true brotherhood was almost a physical feeling wherever I turned. Then our group reached the clerks who examined each passport and suitcase carefully and nodded to the pilgrim to move on.

I was so nervous that when I turned the key in my bag, and it didn't work, I broke open the bag, fearing that they might think I had something in the bag that I shouldn't have. Then the clerk saw that I was handing him an American passport. He held it, he looked at me and said something in Arabic. My friends around me began speaking rapid Arabic, gesturing and pointing, trying to intercede for me. The judge asked me in English for my letter from Dr. Shawarbi, and he thrust it at the clerk, who read it. He gave the letter back, protesting—I could tell that. An argument was going on, about me. I felt like a stupid fool, unable to say a word, I couldn't even understand what was being said. But, finally, sadly, the judge turned to me.

I had to go before the Mabgama Sharia, he explained. It was the Muslim high court which examined all possibly nonauthentic converts to the Islamic religion seeking to enter Mecca. It was absolute that no non-Muslim could enter Mecca. . . . No courts were held on Friday. I would have to wait until Saturday, at least.

An official beckoned a young Arab *mutawwif's* aide. In broken English, the official explained that I would be taken to a place right at the airport. My passport was kept at customs. I wanted to object, because it is a traveler's first law never to get separated from his passport, but I didn't. In my wrapped towels and sandals, I followed the aide in his skullcap, long white gown, and slippers. I guess we were quite a sight. People passing us were speaking all kinds of languages. I couldn't speak anybody's language. I was in bad shape.

Right outside the airport was a mosque, and above the airport was a huge, dormitory-like building, four tiers high. It was semi-dark, not long before dawn, and planes were regularly taking off and landing, their landing lights sweeping the runways or their wing and taillights blinking in the sky. Pilgrims from Ghana, Indonesia, Japan, and Russia, to mention some, were moving to and from the dormitory where I was being taken. I don't believe that motion picture cameras ever have filmed a human spectacle more colorful than my eyes took in. We reached the dormitory and began climbing, up to the fourth, top tier, passing members of every race on earth. Chinese, Indonesians, Afghanis. Many, not yet changed into the *ihram* garb, still wore their national dress. It was like pages out of the *National Geographic* magazine.

My guide, on the fourth tier, gestured me into a compartment that contained about fifteen people. Most lay curled up on their rugs asleep. I could tell that some were women, covered head and foot. An old Russian Muslim and his wife were not asleep. They stared frankly at me. Two Egyptian Muslims and a Persian roused and also stared as my guide moved us over into a corner. With gestures, he indicated that he would demonstrate to me the proper prayer ritual postures. Imagine, being a Muslim minister, a leader in Elijah Muhammad's Nation of Islam, and not knowing the prayer ritual.

I tried to do what he did. I knew I wasn't doing it right. I could feel the other Muslims' eyes on me. Western ankles won't do what Muslim ankles have done for a lifetime. Asians squat when they sit; Westerners sit upright in chairs. When my guide was down in a posture, I tried everything I could to get down as he was, but there I was, sticking up. After about an hour, my guide left, indicating that he would return later.

I never even thought about sleeping. Watched by the Muslims, I kept practicing prayer postures. I refused to let myself think how ridiculous I must have looked to them. After a while, though, I learned a little trick that would let me get down closer to the floor. But after two or three days, my ankle was going to swell.

As the sleeping Muslims woke up, when dawn had broken, they almost instantly became aware of me, and we watched each other while they went about their business. I began to see what an important role the rug played in the overall cultural life of the Muslims. Each individual had a small prayer rug, and each man and wife or large group had a larger communal rug. These Muslims prayed on their rugs there in the compartment. Then they spread a tablecloth over the rug and ate, so the rug became the dining room. Removing the dishes and cloth, they sat on the rug—a living room. Then they curl up and sleep on the rug—a bedroom. In that compartment, before I was to leave it, it dawned on me for the first time why the fence had paid such a high price for Oriental rugs when I had been a burglar in Boston. It was because so much intricate care was taken to weave fine rugs in countries where rugs were so culturally versatile. Later, in Mecca, I would see yet another use of the rug. When any kind of a dispute arose, someone who was respected highly and who was not involved would sit on a rug with the disputers around him, which made the rug a courtroom. In other instances it was a classroom.

One of the Egyptian Muslims, particularly, kept watching me out of the corner of his eye. I smiled at him. He got up and came over to me. "Hel-lo-" he said. It sounded like the Gettysburg Address. I beamed at him, "Hello!" I asked his name. "Name? Name?" He was trying hard, but he didn't get it. We tried some words on each other. I'd guess his English vocabulary spanned maybe twenty words. Just enough to frustrate me. I was trying to get him to comprehend anything. "Sky." I'd point. He'd smile. "Sky," I'd say again, gesturing for him to repeat it after me. He would. "Airplane . . . rug . . . foot . . . sandal . . . eyes. . . ." Like that. Then an amazing thing happened. I was so glad I had some communication with a human being, I was just saying whatever came to mind. I said "Muhammad Ali Clay." All of the Muslims listening lighted up like a Christmas tree. "You? You?" My friend was pointing at me. I shook my head, "No, no. Muhammad Ali Clay my friend—friend!" They half-understood me. Some of them didn't understand, and that's how it began to get around that I was Cassius Clay, world heavyweight champion. I was later to learn that apparently every man, woman, and child in the Muslim world had heard how Sonny Liston (who in the Muslim world had the image of a man-eating ogre) had been beaten in Goliath-David fashion by Cassius Clay, who then had told the world that his name was Muhammad Ali and his religion was Islam and Allah had given him his victory.

Establishing the rapport was the best thing that could have happened in the compartment. My being an American Muslim changed the attitudes from merely watching me to wanting to look out for me. Now, the others began smiling steadily. They came closer; they were frankly looking me up and down. Inspecting me. Very friendly. I was like a man from Mars.

The *mutawwif's* aide returned, indicating that I should go with him.

He pointed from our tier down at the mosque, and I knew that he had come to take me to make the morning prayer, always before sunrise. I followed him down, and we passed pilgrims by the thousands, babbling languages, everything but English. I was angry with myself for not having taken the time to learn more of the orthodox prayer rituals before leaving America. In Elijah Muhammad's Nation of Islam, we hadn't prayed in Arabic. About a dozen or more years before, when I was in prison, a member of the orthodox Muslim movement in Boston, named Abdul Hainid, had visited me and had later sent me prayers in Arabic. At that time, I had learned those prayers phonetically. But I hadn't used them since.

I made up my mind to let the guide do everything first and I would watch him. It wasn't hard to get him to do things first. He wanted to anyway. Just outside the mosque there was a long trough with rows of faucets. Ablutions had to precede praying. I knew that. Even watching the *mutawwif's* helper, I didn't get it right. There's an exact way that an orthodox Muslim washes, and the exact way is very important.

I followed him into the mosque, just a step behind, watching. He did his prostration, his head to the ground. I did mine. "*Bismillah ar-Rahman, ir-Rahman-*" ("In the name of Allah, the Beneficent, the Merciful"). All Muslim prayers began that way. After that, I may not have been mumbling the right thing, but I was mumbling.

I don't mean to have any of this sound joking. It was far from a joke with me. No one who happened to be watching could tell that I wasn't saying what the others said. . . .

LATER THE SAME DAY   I kept standing at the tier railing observing the courtyard below, and I decided to explore a bit on my own. I went down to the first tier. I thought, then, that maybe I shouldn't get too far; someone might come for me. So I went back up to our compartment. In about forty-five minutes, I went back down. I went further this time, feeling my way. I saw a little restaurant in the courtyard. I went straight in there. It was jammed, and babbling with languages. Using gestures, I bought a whole roasted chicken and something like thick potato chips. I got back out in the courtyard, and I tore up that chicken, using my hands. Muslims were doing the same thing all around me. I saw men at least seventy years old bringing both legs up under them, until they made a human knot of themselves, eating with as much aplomb and satisfaction as though they had been in a fine restaurant with waiters all over the place. All ate as One, and slept as One. Everything about the pilgrimage atmosphere accented the Oneness of Man under One God. . . .

I had just said my Sunset Prayer; I was lying on my cot in the fourth-tier compartment, feeling blue and alone when out of the darkness came a sudden light!

It was actually a sudden thought. On one of my venturings in the yard full of activity below, I had noticed four men, officials, seated at a table with a telephone. Now, I thought about seeing them there, and with telephone, my mind flashed to the connection that Dr. Shawarbi in New York had given me the telephone number of the son of the author of the book which had been given to me [in New York]. Omar Azzam lived right there in Jidda!

In a matter of a few minutes, I was downstairs and rushing to where I had seen the four officials. One of them spoke functional English. I excitedly showed him the letter from Dr. Shawarbi. He read it. Then he read it aloud to the other three officials. "A Muslim from America!" I could almost see it capture their imaginations and curiosity. They were very impressed. I asked the English-speaking one if he would please do me the favor of telephoning Dr. Omar Azzam at the number I had. He was glad to do it. He got someone on the phone and conversed in Arabic.

Dr. Omar Azzam came straight to the airport. With the four officials beaming, he wrung my hand in welcome, a young, tall, powerfully built man. I'd say he was six foot three. He had an extremely polished manner. In America, he would have been called a white man, but—it struck me, hard and instantly—from the way he acted, I had no feeling of him being a white man. "Why didn't you call before?" he demanded of me. He showed some identification to the four officials, and he used their phone. Speaking in Arabic, he was talking with some airport officials. "Come!" he said.

In something less than half an hour, he had gotten me released, my suitcase and passport had been retrieved from customs, and we were in Dr. Azzam's car, driving through the city of Jidda, with me dressed in the *ihram* towels and sandals. I was speechless at the man's attitude, and at my own physical feeling of no difference between us as human beings. I had heard for years of Muslim hospitality, but one couldn't quite imagine such warmth. I asked questions. Dr. Azzam was a Swiss-trained engineer. His field was city planning. The Saudi Arabian government had borrowed him from the United Nations to direct all of the reconstruction work being done on the Arabian holy places. And Dr. Azzam's sister was the wife of Prince Faysal's son. I was in a car with the brother-in-law of the son of the ruler of Arabia. Nor was that all that Allah had done. "My father will be so happy to meet you," said Dr. Azzam. The author who had sent me the book!

I asked questions about his father. Abd al-Rahman Azzam was known as Azzam Pasha, or Lord Azzam, until the Egyptian revolution, when President Nasser eliminated all "Lord" and "Noble" titles. "He should be at my home when we get there," Dr. Azzam said. "He spends much time in New York with his United Nations work, and he has followed you with great interest."

I was speechless. . . .

THE HIGH COURT   I learned during dinner that the Hajj Committee Court had been notified about my case, and that in the morning I should be there. And I was.

The Judge was Shaykh Muhammad Harkon. The court was empty except for me and a sister from India, formerly a Protestant, who had converted to Islam and was, like me, trying to make the Hajj. She was brown skinned, with a small face that was mostly covered. Judge Harkon was a kind, impressive man. We talked. He asked me some questions having to do with my sincerity. I answered him as truly as I could. He not only recognized me as a true Muslim, but he gave me two books, one in English, the other in Arabic. He recorded my name in the Holy Register of true Muslims, and we were ready to part. He told me, "I hope you will become a great preacher of Islam in America." I said that I shared that hope, and I would try to fulfill it.

The Azzam family were very elated that I was qualified and accepted to go to Mecca. I had lunch at the Jidda Palace Hotel. Then I slept again for several hours, until the telephone awakened me.

It was Muhammad Abd al-Azziz Magid, the Deputy Chief of Protocol for Prince Faysal. "A special car will be waiting to take you to Mecca, right after your dinner," he told me. He advised me to eat heartily, as the Hajj rituals require plenty of strength.

I was beyond astonishment by then.

Two young Arabs accompanied me to Mecca. A well-lighted, modern turnpike highway made the trip easy. Guards at intervals along the way took one look at the car, and the driver made a sign, and we were passed through, never even having to slow down. I was, all at once, thrilled, important, humble, and thankful.

Mecca, when we entered, seemed as ancient as time itself. Our car slowed through the winding streets, lined by shops on both sides and with buses, cars, and trucks, and tens of thousands of pilgrims from all over the earth were everywhere.

The car halted briefly at a place where a *mutawwif* was waiting for me. He wore the white skullcap and long nightshirt garb that I had seen at the airport. He was a short, dark-skinned Arab, named Muhammad. He spoke no English whatever.

We parked near the Great Mosque. We performed our ablution and entered. Pilgrims seemed to be on top of each other, there were so many, lying, sitting, sleeping, praying, walking.

My vocabulary cannot describe the new mosque that was being built around the Ka'ba. I was thrilled to realize that it was only one of the tremendous rebuilding tasks under the direction of young Dr. Azzam, who had just been my host. The Great Mosque of Mecca, when it is finished, will surpass the architectural beauty of India's Taj Mahal.

Carrying my sandals, I followed the *mutawwif.* Then I saw the Ka'ba, a huge black stone house in the middle of the Great Mosque. It was being circumambulated by thousands upon thousands of praying pilgrims, both sexes, and every size, shape, color, and race in the world. I knew the prayer to be uttered when the pilgrim's eyes first perceive the Ka'ba. Translated, it is "O God, you are peace, and peace derives from you. So greet us, O Lord, with peace." . . .

My feeling there in the House of God was a numbness. My *mutawwif* led me in the crowd of praying, chanting pilgrims, moving seven times around the Ka'ba. Some were bent and wizened with age; it was a sight that stamped itself on the brain. I saw incapacitated pilgrims being carried by others. Faces were enraptured in their faith. The seventh time around, I prayed two rakats, prostrating myself, my head on the floor. The first prostration, I prayed the Quran verse "Say he is God, the one and only"; the second prostration, "Say O you who are unbelievers, I worship not that which you worship. . . ."

As I prostrated, the *mutawwif* fended pilgrims off to keep me from being trampled.

The *mutawwif* and I next drank water from the Well of Zamzam. Then we ran between the two hills, Safa and Marwa, where Hagar wandered over the same earth searching for water for her child, Ishmael.

THE PROCESSION TO ARAFAT   Three separate times after that, I visited the Great Mosque, and circumambulated the Ka'ba. The next day we set out after sunrise toward Mount Arafat, thousands of us, crying in unison: "*Labayk! Labayk!*" and "*Allah Akbar!*" Mecca is surrounded by the crudest-looking mountains I have ever seen; they seem to be made of the slag from a blast furnace. No vegetation is on them at all. Arriving about noon, we prayed and chanted from noon until sunset, and the *asr* (afternoon) and *maghrib* (sunset) special prayers were performed.

Finally, we lifted our hands in prayer and thanksgiving, repeating Allah's words: "There is no God but Allah. He has no partner. His are authority and praise. Good emanates from him, and he has power over all things."

Standing on Mount Arafat had concluded the essential rites of being a pilgrim to Mecca. No one who missed it could consider himself a pilgrim.

The *ihram* had ended. We cast the traditional seven stones at the devil. Some had their hair and beards cut. I decided that I was going to let my beard remain. I wondered what my wife, Betty, and our little daughters were going to say when they saw me with a beard, when I got back to New York. New York seemed a million miles away. I hadn't seen a newspaper that I could read since I left New York. I had no idea what was happening there. A Negro rifle club that had been in existence for over twelve years in Harlem had been "discovered" by the police; it was being trumpeted that I was "behind it." Elijah Muhammad's Nation of Islam had a lawsuit going against me, to force me and my family to vacate the house in which we lived on Long Island.

The major press, radio, and television media in America had representatives in Cairo hunting all over, trying to locate me, to interview me about the furor in New York that I had allegedly caused—when I knew nothing about any of it. . . .

LETTERS FROM MECCA   I wrote to Dr. Shawarbi, whose belief in my sincerity had enabled me to get a passport to Mecca.

All through the night, I copied similar long letters for others who were very close to me. Among them was Elijah Muhammad's son Wallace Muhammad, who had expressed to me his conviction that the only possible salvation for the Nation of Islam would be its accepting and projecting a better understanding of orthodox Islam.

And I wrote to my loyal assistants at my newly formed Muslim

Mosque, Inc., in Harlem, with a note appended, asking that my letter be duplicated and distributed to the press.

I knew that when my letter became public knowledge back in America, many would be astounded—loved ones, friends, and enemies alike. And no less astounded would be millions whom I did not know who had gained during my twelve years with Elijah Muhammad a "hate" image of Malcolm X.

Even I was myself astounded. But there was precedent in my life for this letter. My whole life had been a chronology of—*changes.*

Here is what I wrote . . . from my heart:

"Never have I witnessed such sincere hospitality and the overwhelming spirit of true brotherhood as is practiced by people of all colors and races here in this ancient Holy Land, the home of Abraham, Muhammad, and all the other prophets of the Holy Scriptures. For the past week, I have been utterly speechless and spellbound by the graciousness I see displayed all around me by people *of all colors.*

"I have been blessed to visit the Holy City of Mecca. I have made my seven circuits around the Ka'ba, led by a young *mutawwif* named Muhammad. I drank water from the Well of Zamzam. I ran seven times back and forth between the hills of Mount Safa and Marwa. I have prayed in the ancient city of Mina, and I have prayed on Mount Arafat.

"There were tens of thousands of pilgrims, from all over the world. They were of all colors, from blue-eyed blonds to black-skinned Africans. But we were all participating in the same ritual, displaying a spirit of unity and brotherhood that my experiences in America had led me to believe never could exist between the white and the nonwhite.

"America needs to understand Islam, because this is the one religion that erases from its society the race problem. Throughout my travels in the Muslim world, I have met, talked to, and even eaten with people who in America would have been considered 'white'—but the 'white' attitude was removed from their minds by the religion of Islam. I have never before seen *sincere* and *true* brotherhood practiced by all colors together, irrespective of their color.

"You may be shocked by these words coming from me. But on this pilgrimage, what I have seen, and experienced, has forced me to *rearrange* much of my thought patterns previously held, and to *toss aside* some of my previous conclusions. This was not too difficult for me. Despite my firm convictions, I have always been a man who tries to face facts, and to accept the reality of life as new experience and new knowledge unfolds it. I have always kept an open mind, which is necessary to the flexibility that must go hand in hand with every form of intelligent search for truth.

"During the past eleven days here in the Muslim world, I have eaten from the same plate, drunk from the same glass, and slept in the same bed (or on the same rug)—while praying to the *same God*—with fellow Muslims, whose eyes were the bluest of blue, whose hair was the blondest of blond, and whose skin was the whitest of white. And in the words and in the actions and in the *deeds* of the 'white' Muslims, I felt the same sincerity that I felt among the black African Muslims of Nigeria, Sudan, and Ghana.

"We were *truly* all the same (brothers)—because their belief in one God had removed the 'white' from their minds, the 'white' from their *behavior*, and the 'white' from their *attitude*. . . ."

THE MUSLIM FROM AMERICA   Prince Faysal, the absolute ruler of Arabia, had made me a guest of the state. Among the courtesies and privileges which this brought to me, especially—shamelessly—I relished the chauffeured car which toured me around in Mecca with the chauffeur-guide pointing out sights of particular significance. Some of the Holy City looked as ancient as time itself. Other parts of it resembled a modern Miami suburb. I cannot describe with what feelings I actually pressed my hands against the earth where the great prophets had trod four thousand years before.

"The Muslim from America" excited everywhere the most intense curiosity and interest. I was mistaken time and again for Cassius Clay. A local newspaper had printed a photograph of Cassius and me together at the United Nations. Through my chauffeur-guide-interpreter I was asked scores of questions about Cassius. Even children knew of him, and loved him there in the Muslim world. By popular demand, the cinemas throughout Africa and Asia had shown his fight. At that moment in young Cassius's career, he had captured the imagination and the support of the entire dark world.

My car took me to participate in special prayers at Mount Arafat, and at Mina. The roads offered the wildest drives that I had ever known: nightmare traffic, brakes squealing, skidding cars, and horns blowing. (I believe that all of the driving in the Holy Land is done in the name of Allah.) I had begun to learn the prayers in Arabic; now, my biggest prayer difficulty was physical. The unaccustomed prayer posture had caused my big toe to swell, and it pained me.

But the Muslim world's customs no longer seemed strange to me. My hands now readily plucked up food from a common dish shared with brother Muslims; I was drinking without hesitation from the same glass as others; I was washing from the same little pitcher of water; and sleeping with eight or ten others on a mat in the open. I remember one night at Muzdalifa with nothing but the sky overhead I lay awake amid sleeping Muslim brothers and I learned that pilgrims from every land—every color, and class, and rank; high officials and the beggar alike—all snored in the same language. . . .

It was the largest Hajj in history, I was later told. Kasem Gulek, of the Turkish parliament, beaming with pride, informed me that from Turkey alone over six hundred buses—over fifty thousand Muslims—had made the pilgrimage. I told him that I dreamed to see the day when shiploads and planeloads of American Muslims would come to Mecca for the Hajj.

There was a color pattern in the huge crowds. Once I happened to notice this, I closely observed it thereafter. Being from America made me intensely sensitive to matters of color. I saw that people who looked alike drew together and most of the time stayed together. This was entirely voluntary; there being no other reason for it. But Africans were with Africans. Pakistanis were with Pakistanis. And so on. I tucked it into my mind that when I returned home I would tell Americans this observation; that where true brotherhood existed among all colors, where no one felt segregated, where there was no "superiority" complex, no 'inferiority" complex—then voluntarily, naturally, people of the same kind felt drawn together by that which they had in common. . . .

Constantly, wherever I went, I was asked questions about America's racial discrimination. Even with my background, I was astonished at the degree to which the major single image of America seemed to be discrimination.

In a hundred different conversations in the Holy Land with Muslims high and low, and from around the world—and, later, when I got to black Africa—I don't have to tell you never once did I bite my tongue or miss a single opportunity to tell the truth about the crimes, the evils, and the indignities that are suffered by the black man in America. Through my interpreter, I lost no opportunity to advertise the American black man's real plight. I preached it on the mountain at Arafat, I preached it in the busy lobby of the Jidda Palace Hotel. I would point at one after another— to bring it closer to home; "You . . . you . . . you—because of your dark skin, in America you, too, would be called 'Negro.' You could be bombed and shot and cattle-prodded and fire-hosed and beaten because of your complexions."

As some of the poorest pilgrims heard me preach, so did some of the Holy World's most important personages. I talked at length with the blue-eyed, blond-haired Husayn Amini, Grand Mufti of Jerusalem. We were introduced on Mount Arafat by Kasem Gulek of the Turkish parliament. Both were learned men; both were especially well read on America. Kasem Gulek asked me why I had broken with Elijah Muhammad. I said that I preferred not to elaborate upon our differences, in the interests of preserving the American black man's unity. They both understood and accepted that.

I talked with the Mayor of Mecca, Shaykh Abdullah Eraif, who when he was a journalist had criticized the methods of the Mecca municipality and Prince Faysal made him the Mayor to see if he could do any better. Everyone generally acknowledged that Shaykh Eraif was doing fine. A filmed feature *The Muslim from America* was made by Ahmed Horyallah and his partner, Essid Muhammad, of Tunis's television station. In America once, in Chicago, Ahmed Horyallah had interviewed Elijah Muhammad.

The lobby of the Jidda Palace Hotel offered me frequent sizable informal audiences of important men from many different countries who were curious to hear the "American Muslim." I met many Africans who had either spent some time in America or who had heard other Africans' testimony about America's treatment of the black man. I remember how before one large audience, one cabinet minister from black Africa (he knew more about worldwide current events than anyone else I've ever met) told of his occasionally traveling in the United States, North and South, deliberately not wearing his national dress. Just recalling the indignities he had met as a black man seemed to expose some raw nerve in this highly educated, dignified official. His eyes blazed in his passionate anger, his hands hacked the air: "Why is the American black man so complacent about being trampled upon? Why doesn't the American black man *fight* to be a human being?" . . .

Two American authors, best-sellers in the Holy Land, had helped to spread and intensify the concern for the American black man. James Baldwin's books, translated, had made a tremendous impact, as had the book *Black Like Me*, by John Griffin. If you're unfamiliar with that book, it tells how the white man Griffin blackened his skin and spent two months traveling as a Negro about America; then Griffin wrote of the experiences that he met. "A frightening experience!" I heard exclaimed many times by people in the Holy World who had read the popular book. But I never heard it without opening their thinking further: "Well, if it was a frightening experience for him as nothing but a make-believe Negro for sixty days—then you think about what *real* Negroes in America have gone through for four hundred years."

INTERVIEW WITH FAYSAL   One honor that came to me, I had prayed for: His Eminence, Prince Faysal, invited me to a personal audience with him.

As I entered the room, tall, handsome Prince Faysal came from behind his desk. I never will forget the reflection I had at that instant, that here was one of the world's most important men, and yet with his dignity one saw clearly his sincere humility. He indicated for me a chair opposite from his. Our interpreter was the Deputy Chief of Protocol, Muhammad Abdal-Azziz Magid, an Egyptian-born Arab who looked like a Harlem Negro.

Prince Faysal impatiently gestured when I began stumbling for words trying to express my gratitude for the great honor he had paid me in making me a guest of the state. It was only Muslim hospitality to another Muslim, he explained, and I was an unusual Muslim from America. He asked me to understand above all that whatever he had done had been his pleasure, with no other motives whatever.

A gliding servant served a choice of two kinds of tea as Prince Faysal talked. His son, Muhammad Faysal, had "met" me on American television while attending a northern California university. Prince Faysal had read Egyptian writers' articles about the American "Black Muslims." "If what these writers say is true, the Black Muslims have the wrong Islam," he said. I explained my role of the previous twelve years, of helping to organize and to build the Nation of Islam. I said that my purpose for making the Hajj was to get an understanding of true Islam. "That is good," Prince Faysal said, pointing out that there was an abundance of English-translation literature about Islam—so that there was no excuse for ignorance, and no reason for sincere people to allow themselves to be misled.

ALICE   WALKER

LOOKING FOR ZORA

On January 16, 1959, Zora Neale Hurston, suffering from the effects of a stroke and writing painfully in longhand, composed a letter to the "editorial department" of Harper & Brothers inquiring if they would be interested in seeing "the book I am laboring upon at present—a life of Herod the Great." One year and twelve days later, Zora Neale Hurston died without funds to provide for her burial, a resident of the St. Lucie County, Florida, Welfare Home. She lies today in an unmarked grave in a segregated cemetery in Pierce, Florida, a resting place generally symbolic of the black writer's fate in America.

Zora Neale Hurston is one of the most significant unread authors in America, the author of two minor classics and four other major books.

—Robert Hemenway, "Zora Hurston and the Eatonville
Anthropology" in *The Harlem Renaissance Remembered*

n August 15, 1973, I wake up just as the plane is lowering over Sanford, Florida, which means I am also looking down on Eatonville, Zora Neale Hurston's birthplace. I recognize it from Zora's description in *Mules and Men*: "the city of five lakes, three croquet courts, three hundred brown skins, three hundred good swimmers, plenty guavas, two schools, and no jailhouse." Of course I cannot see the guavas, but the five lakes are still there, and it is the lakes I count as the plane prepares to land in Orlando.

From the air, Florida looks completely flat, and as we near the ground this impression does not change. This is the first time I have seen the interior of the state, which Zora wrote about so well, but there are the acres of orange groves, the sand, mangrove trees, and scrub pine that I know from her books. Getting off the plane I walk through the humid air of midday into the tacky but air-conditioned airport. I search for Charlotte Hunt, my companion on the Zora Hurston expedition. She lives in Winter Park, Florida, very near Eatonville, and is writing her graduate dissertation on Zora. I see her waving—a large, pleasant-faced white woman in dark glasses. We have written to each other for several weeks, swapping our latest finds (mostly hers) on Zora, and trying to make sense out of the mass of information obtained (often erroneous or simply confusing) from Zora herself—through her stories and autobiography—and from people who wrote about her.

Eatonville has lived for such a long time in my imagination that I can hardly believe it will be found existing in its own right. But after twenty minutes on the expressway, Charlotte turns off and I see a small settlement of houses and stores set with no particular pattern in the sandy soil off the road. We stop in front of a neat gray building that has two fascinating signs: EATONVILLE POST OFFICE and EATONVILLE CITY HALL.

Inside the Eatonville City Hall half of the building, a slender, dark-brown-skin woman sits looking through letters on a desk. When she hears we are searching for anyone who might have known Zora Neale Hurston, she leans back in thought. Because I don't wish to inspire foot-dragging in people who might know something about Zora they're not sure they should tell, I have decided on a simple, but I feel profoundly *useful* lie.

"I am Miss Hurston's niece," I prompt the young woman, who brings her head down with a smile.

"I think Mrs. Moseley is about the only one still living who might remember her," she says.

"Do you mean *Mathilda* Moseley, the woman who tells those 'woman-is-smarter-than-man' lies in Zora's book?"

"Yes," says the young woman. "Mrs. Moseley is real old now, of course. But this time of day, she should be at home." I stand at the counter looking down on her, the first Eatonville resident I have spoken to. Because of Zora's books, I feel I know something about her; at least I know what the town she grew up in was like years before she was born.

"Tell me something." I say, "Do the schools teach Zora's books here?"

"No," she says, "they don't. I don't think most people know anything about Zora Neale Hurston, or know about any of the great things she did. She was a fine lady. I've read all of her books myself, but I don't think many other folks in Eatonville have."

"Many of the church people around here, as I understand it," says Charlotte in a murmured aside, "thought Zora was pretty loose. I don't think they appreciated her writing about them."

"Well," I say to the young woman, "thank you for your help." She clarifies her directions to Mrs. Moseley's house and smiles as Charlotte and I turn to go.

The letter to Harper's does not expose a publisher's rejection of an unknown masterpiece, but it does reveal how the bright promise of the Harlem Renaissance deteriorated for many of the writers who shared in its exuberance. It also indicates the personal tragedy of Zora Neale Hurston: Barnard graduate, author of four novels, two books of folklore, one volume of autobiography, the most important collector of Afro-American folklore in America, reduced by poverty and circumstance to seek a publisher by unsolicited mail.

—Robert Hemenway

Zora Hurston was born in 1901, 1902, or 1903—depending on how old she felt herself to be at the time someone asked.

—Librarian, Beinecke Library, Yale University

The Moseley house is small and white and snug, its yard nearly swallowed up by oleanders and hibiscus bushes. Charlotte and I knock on the door. I call out but there is no answer. This strikes us as peculiar. We have had time to figure out an age for Mrs. Moseley—not dates or a number, just old. I am thinking of a quivery, bedridden invalid when we hear the car. We look behind us to see an old black-and-white Buick—paint peeling and grillwork rusty—pulling into the drive. A neat old lady in a purple dress and with white hair is straining at the wheel. She is frowning because Charlotte's car is in the way.

Mrs. Moseley looks at us suspiciously. "Yes, I knew Zora Neale," she says, unsmilingly and with a rather cold stare at Charlotte (who, I imagine, feels very *white* at that moment), "but that was a long time ago, and I don't want to talk about it."

"Yes ma'am," I murmur, bringing all my sympathy to bear on the situation.

"Not only that," Mrs. Moseley continues, "I've been sick. Been in the hospital for an operation. Ruptured artery. The doctors didn't believe I was going to live, but you see me alive, don't you?"

"Looking well, too," I comment.

Mrs. Moseley is out of her car. A thin, sprightly woman with nice gold-studded false teeth, uppers and lowers. I like her because she stands there *straight* beside her car, with a hand on her hip and her straw pocketbook on her arm. She wears white T-strap shoes with heels that show off her well-shaped legs.

"I'm eighty-two years old, you know," she says. "And I just can't remember things the way I used to. Anyhow, Zora Neale left here to go to school and she never really came back to live. She'd come here for material for her books, but that was all. She spent most of her time down in South Florida."

"You know, Mrs. Moseley, I saw your name in one of Zora's books."

"You did?" She looks at me with only slightly more interest. "I read some of her books a long time ago, but then people got to borrowing and borrowing and they borrowed them all away."

"I could send you a copy of everything that's been printed," I offer. "Would you like me to do that?"

"No," says Mrs. Moseley promptly, "I don't read much anymore. Besides, all of that was so long ago. . . ."

Charlotte and I settle back against the car in the sun. Mrs. Moseley tells us at length and with exact recall every step in her recent operation, ending with: "What those doctors didn't know—when they were expecting me to die (and they didn't even think I'd live long enough for them to have to take stitches!)—is that Jesus is the best doctor, and if *He* says to get well, that's all that counts."

With this philosophy, Charlotte and I murmur assent—being Southerners and church bred, we have heard that belief before. But what we learn from Mrs. Moseley is that she does not remember much beyond the year 1938. She shows us a picture of her father and mother and says that her father was Joe Clarke's brother. Joe Clarke, as every Zora Hurston reader knows, was the first mayor of Eatonville; his fictional counterpart is Jody Starks of *Their Eyes Were Watching God.* We also get directions to where Joe Clarke's store was—where Club Eaton is now. Club Eaton, a long orange-beige nightspot we had seen on the main road, is apparently famous for the good times in it regularly had by all. It is, perhaps, the modern equivalent of the store porch, where all the men of Zora's childhood came to tell "lies," that is, black folk tales, that were "made and used on the spot," to take a line from Zora. As for Zora's exact birthplace, Mrs. Moseley has no idea.

After I have commented on the healthy growth of her hibiscus bushes, she becomes more talkative. She mentions how much she loved to dance, when she was a young woman, and talks about how good her husband was. When he was alive, she says, she was completely happy because he allowed her to be completely free. "I was so free I had to pinch myself sometimes to tell if I was a married woman."

Relaxed now, she tells us about going to school with Zora. "Zora and I went to the same school. It's called Hungerford High now. It was only to the eighth grade. But our teachers were so good that by the time you left you knew college subjects. When I went to Morris Brown in Atlanta, the teachers there were just teaching me the same things I had already learned right in Eatonville. I wrote Mama and told her I was going to come home and help her with her babies. I wasn't learning anything new."

"Tell me something, Mrs. Moseley," I ask. "Why do you suppose Zora was against integration? I read somewhere that she was against school desegregation because she felt it was an insult to black teachers."

"Oh, one of them [white people] come around asking me about integration. One day I was doing shopping. I heard 'em over there talking about it in the store, about the schools. And I got on out of the way because I knew if they asked me, they wouldn't like what I was going to tell 'em. But they came up and asked me anyhow. 'What do you think about this integration?' one of them said. I acted like I thought I had heard wrong. 'You're asking *me* what I think about integration?' I said. 'Well, as you can see, I'm just an old colored woman'—seventy-five or seventy-six then—'and this is the first time anybody ever asked me about integration. And nobody asked my grandmother what she thought, either, but her daddy was one of you all.'" Mrs. Moseley seems satisfied with this memory of her rejoinder. She looks at Charlotte. "I have the blood of three races in my veins," she says belligerently, "white, black, and Indian, and nobody asked me *anything* before."

"Do you think living in Eatonville made integration less appealing to you?"

"Well, I can tell you this: I have lived in Eatonville all my life, and I've been in the governing of this town. I've been everything but mayor and I've been assistant mayor. Eatonville was and is an all-black town. We have our own police department, post office, and town hall. Our own school and good teachers. Do I need integration?

"They took over Goldsboro, because the black people who lived there never incorporated, like we did. And now I don't even know if any black folks live there. They built big houses up there around the lakes. But we didn't let that happen in Eatonville, and we don't sell land to just anybody. And you see, we're still here."

When we leave, Mrs. Moseley is standing by her car, waving. I think of the letter Roy Wilkins wrote to a black newspaper blasting Zora Neale for her lack of enthusiasm about the integration of schools. I wonder if he knew the experience of Eatonville she was coming from. Not many black people in America have come from a self-contained, all-black community where loyalty and unity are taken for granted. A place where black pride is nothing new.

There is, however, one thing Mrs. Moseley said that bothered me.

"Tell me, Mrs. Moseley," I had asked, "why is it that thirteen years after Zora's death, no marker has been put on her grave?"

And Mrs. Moseley answered: "The reason she doesn't have a stone is because she wasn't buried here. She was buried down in South Florida somewhere. I don't think anybody really knew where she was."

Only to reach a wider audience, need she ever write books—because she is a perfect book of entertainment in herself. In her youth she was always getting scholarships and things from wealthy white people, some of whom simply paid her just to sit around and represent the Negro race for them, she did it in such a racy fashion. She was full of sidesplitting anecdotes, humorous tales, and tragicomic stories, remembered out of her life in the South as a daughter of a traveling minister of God. She could make you laugh one minute and cry the next. To many of her white friends, no doubt, she was a perfect "darkie," in the nice meaning they give the term—that is, a naive, childlike, sweet, humorous, and highly colored Negro.

But Miss Hurston was clever, too—a student who didn't let college give her a broad "a" and who had great scorn for all pretensions, academic or otherwise. That is why she was such a fine folklore collector, able to go among the people and never act as if she had been to school at all. Almost nobody else could stop the average Harlemite on Lenox Avenue and measure his head with a strange-looking, anthropological device and not get bawled out for the attempt, except Zora, who used to stop anyone whose head looked interesting, and measure it.

—Langston Hughes, *The Big Sea*

What does it matter what white folks must have thought about her?

—Student, black women writers class, Wellesley College

Mrs. Sarah Peek Patterson is a handsome, red-haired woman in her late forties, wearing orange slacks and gold earrings. She is the director of Lee-Peek Mortuary in Fort Pierce, the establishment that handled Zora's burial. Unlike most black funeral homes in Southern towns that sit like palaces among the general poverty, Lee-Peek has a rundown, *small* look. Perhaps this is because it is painted purple and white, as are its Cadillac chariots. These colors do not age well. The rooms are cluttered and grimy, and the bathroom is a tiny, stale-smelling prison, with a bottle of black hair dye (apparently used to touch up the hair of the corpses) dripping into the face bowl. Two pine burial boxes are resting in the bathtub.

Mrs. Patterson herself is pleasant and helpful.

"As I told you over the phone, Mrs. Patterson," I begin, shaking her hand and looking into her penny-brown eyes, "I am Zora Neale Hurston's niece, and I would like to have a marker put on her grave. You said, when I called you last week, that you could tell me where the grave is."

By this time I am, of course, completely into being Zora's niece, and the lie comes with perfect naturalness to my lips. Besides, as far as I'm concerned, she is my aunt—and that of all black people as well.

"She was buried in 1960," exclaims Mrs. Patterson. "That was when my father was running this funeral home. He's sick now or I'd let you talk to him. But I know where she's buried. She's in the old cemetery, the Garden of the Heavenly Rest, on Seventeenth Street. Just when you go in the gate there's a circle and she's buried right in the middle of it. Hers is the only grave in that circle—because people don't bury in that cemetery any more.

She turns to a stocky, black-skinned woman in her thirties wearing a green polo shirt and white jeans cut off at the knee. "This lady will show you where it is," she says.

"I can't tell you how much I appreciate this," I say to Mrs. Patterson, as I rise to go. "And could you tell me something else? You see, I never met my aunt. When she died, I was still a junior in high school. But could you tell me what she died of, and what kind of funeral she had?"

"I don't know exactly what she died of," Mrs. Patterson says. "I know she didn't have any money. Folks took up a collection to bury her. . . . I believe she died of malnutrition."

"Malnutrition?"

Outside, in the blistering sun, I lean my head against Charlotte's even more blistering car top. The sting of the hot metal only intensifies my anger. "Malnutrition," I manage to mutter. "Hell, our condition hasn't changed *any* since Phillis Wheatley's time. She died of malnutrition!"

"Really?" says Charlotte. "I didn't know that."

One cannot overemphasize the extent of her commitment. It was so great that her marriage in 1927 to Herbert Sheen was short-lived. Although divorce did not come officially until 1931—the two separated amicably after only a few months—Hurston to continue her collecting, Sheen to attend medical school. Hurston never married again.

—Robert Hemenway

"What is your name?" I ask the woman who has climbed into the back seat.

"Rosalee," she says. She has a rough, pleasant voice, as if she be a singer who also smokes a lot. She is homely and has an air of ready indifference.

"Another woman came by here wanting to see the grave," she says, lighting up a cigarette. "She was a little short, dumpy white lady from one of these Florida schools. Orlando or Daytona. But let me tell you something before we gets started. All I know is where the cemetery is. I don't know one thing about that grave. You better go back in and ask her to draw you a map."

A few moments later, with Mrs. Patterson's diagram of where the grave is, we head for the cemetery.

We drive past blocks of small, pastel-colored houses and turn right onto Seventeenth Street. At the very end, we reach a tall curving gate, with the words GARDEN OF THE HEAVENLY REST fading into the stone. I expected, from Mrs. Patterson's small drawing, to find a small circle— which would have placed Zora's grave five or ten paces from the road. But the "circle" is over an acre large and looks more like an abandoned field. Tall weeds choke the dirt road and scrape against the sides of the car. It doesn't help either that I step out into an active ant hill.

"I don't know about y'all," I say, "but I don't even believe this." I am used to the haphazard cemetery-keeping that is traditional in most Southern black communities, but this neglect is staggering. As far as I can see there is nothing but bushes and weeds, some as tall as my waist. One grave is near the road and Charlotte elects to investigate it. It is fairly clean, and belongs to someone who died in 1963.

Rosalee and I plunge into the weeds; I pull my long dress up to my hips. The weeds scratch my knees, and the insects have a feast. Looking back, I see Charlotte standing resolutely near the road.

"Aren't you coming?" I call.

"No," she calls back. "I'm from these parts and I know what's out there." She means snakes.

"Shit," I say, my whole life and the people I love flashing melodramatically before my eyes. Rosalee is a few yards to my right.

"How're you going to find anything out here?" she asks. And I stand still a few seconds, looking at the weeds. Some of them are quite pretty, with tiny yellow flowers. They are thick and healthy, but dead weeds under them have formed a thick, gray carpet on the ground. A snake could be lying six inches from my big toe and I wouldn't see it. We move slowly, very slowly, our eyes alert, our legs trembly. It is hard to tell where the center of the circle is since the circle is not really round, but more like half of something round. There are things crackling and hissing in the grass. Sandspurs are sticking to the inside of my skirt. Sand and ants cover my feet. I look toward the road and notice that there are, indeed, *two* large curving stones, making an entrance and exit to the cemetery. I take my bearing from them and try to navigate to exact center. But the center of anything can be very large, and a grave is not a pinpoint. Finding the grave seems positively hopeless. There is only one thing to do.

"Zora!" I yell, as loud as I can (causing Rosalee to jump). "Are you out here?"

"If she is, I sho hope she don't answer you. If she do, I'm gone."

"Zora," I call again. "I'm here. Are you?"

"If she is," grumbles Rosalee, "I hope she'll keep it to herself."

"Zora!" Then I start fussing with her. "I hope you don't think I'm going to stand out here all day, with these snakes watching me and these ants having a field day. In fact, I'm going to call you just one or two more times." On a clump of dried grass, near a small bushy tree, my eye falls on one of the largest bugs I have ever seen. It is on its back, and is as large as three of my fingers. I walk toward it, and yell "Zo-ra!" and my foot sinks into a hole. I look down. I am standing in a sunken rectangle that is about six feet long and about three or four feet wide. I look up to see where the two gates are.

"Well," I say, "this is the center, or approximately anyhow. It's also the only sunken spot we've found. Doesn't this look like a grave to you?"

"For the sake of not going no farther through these bushes," Rosalee growls, "yes, it do."

"Wait a minute," I say, "I have to look around some more to be sure this is the only spot that resembles a grave. But you don't have to come."

Rosalee smiles—a grin, really—beautiful and tough.

"Naw," she says, "I feels sorry for you. If one of these snakes got ahold of you out here by yourself I'd feel *real* bad." She laughs. "I done come this far, I'll go on with you."

"Thank you, Rosalee," I say. "Zora thanks you too."

"Just as long as she don't try to tell me in person," she says and together we walk down the field.

The gusto and flavor of Zora Neal[e] Hurston's storytelling, for example, long before the yarns were published in "Mules and Men" and other books, became a local legend which might . . . have spread further under different conditions. A tiny shift in the center of gravity could have made them best-sellers.

—Ama Bontemps, *Personals*

Bitter over the rejection of her folklore's value, especially in the black community, frustrated by what she felt was her failure to convert the Afro-American world view into the forms of prose fiction, Hurston finally gave up.

—Robert Hemenway

When Charlotte and I drive up to the Merritt Monument Company, I immediately see the headstone I want.

"How much is this one?" I ask the young woman in charge, pointing to a tall black stone. It looks as majestic as Zora herself must have been when she was learning voodoo from those root doctors down in New Orleans.

"Oh, that one," she says, "that's our finest. That's Ebony Mist."

"Well, how much is it?"

"I don't know. But wait," she says, looking around in relief, "here comes somebody who'll know."

A small, sunburned man with squinty green eyes comes up. He must be the engraver, I think, because his eyes are contracted into slits, as if he has been keeping stone dust out of them for years.

"That's Ebony Mist," he says. "That's our best."

"How much is it?" I ask, beginning to realize I probably *can't* afford it.

He gives me a price that would feed a dozen Sahelian drought victims for three years. I realize that I must honor the dead, but between the dead great and the living starving, there is no choice.

"I have a lot of letters to be engraved," I say, standing by the plain gray marker I have chosen. It is pale and ordinary, not at all like Zora, and makes me momentarily angry that I am not rich.

We go into his office and I hand him a sheet of paper that has:

ZORA NEALE HURSTON

"A GENIUS OF THE SOUTH"

NOVELIST FOLKWRITER

ANTHROPOLOGIST

1901   1960

"A genius of the South" is from one of Jean Toomer's poems.

"Where is this grave?" the monument man asks. "If it's in a new cemetery, the stone has to be flat."

"Well, it's not a new cemetery and Zora—my aunt—doesn't need anything flat, because with the weeds out there, you'd never be able to see it. You'll have to go out there with me."

He grunts.

"And take a long pole and 'sound' the spot." I add. "Because there's no way of telling it's a grave, except that it's sunken."

"Well," he says, after taking my money and writing up a receipt, in the full awareness that he's the only monument dealer for miles, "you take this flag" (he hands me a four-foot-long pole with a red-metal marker on top) "and take it out to the cemetery and put it where you think the grave is. It'll take us about three weeks to get the stone out there."

I wonder if be knows he is sending me to another confrontation with the snakes. He probably does. Charlotte has told me she will cut my leg and suck out the blood if I am bit.

"At least send me a photograph when it's done, won't you?"

He says he will.

Hurston's return to her folklore-collecting in December of 1927 was made possible by Mrs. R. Osgood Mason, an elderly white patron of the arts, who at various times also helped Langston Hughes, Alain Locke, Richmond Barthe, and Miguel Covarrubias. Hurston apparently came to her attention through the intercession of Locke, who frequently served as a kind of liaison between the young black talent and Mrs. Mason. The entire relationship between this woman and the Harlem Renaissance deserves extended study, for it represents much of the ambiguity involved in white patronage of black artists. All her artists were instructed to call her "Godmother"; there was a decided emphasis on the "primitive" aspects of black culture, apparently a holdover from Mrs. Mason's interest in the Plains Indians. In Hurston's case there were special restrictions imposed by her patron—although she was to be paid a handsome salary for her folklore collecting, she was to limit her correspondence and publish nothing of her research without prior approval.

—Robert Hemenway

You have to read the chapters Zora *left out* of her autobiography.

—Student Special Collections Room,
Beinecke Library, Yale University

Dr. Benton, a friend of Zora's and a practicing M.D. in Fort Pierce, is one of those old, good-looking men whom I always have trouble not liking. (It no longer bothers me that I may be constantly searching for father figures; by this time, I have found several and dearly enjoyed knowing them all.) He is shrewd, with steady brown eyes under hair that is almost white. He is probably in his seventies, but doesn't look it. He carries himself with dignity, and has cause to be proud of the new clinic where he now practices medicine. His nurse looks at us with suspicion, but Dr. Benton's eyes have the penetration of a scalpel cutting through skin. I guess right away that if he knew anything about Zora Hurston, he will not believe I am her niece. "Eatonville?" Dr. Benton says, leaning forward in his chair, looking first at me, then at Charlotte. "Yes, I know Eatonville; I grew up not far from there. I knew the whole bunch of Zora's family." (He looks at the shape of my cheekbones, the size of my eyes, and the nappiness of my hair.) "I knew her daddy. The old man. He was a hard-working Christian man. Did the best he could for his family. He was the mayor of Eatonville for a while, you know."

"My father was the mayor of Goldsboro. You probably never heard of it. It never incorporated like Eatonville did, and has just about disappeared. But Eatonville is still all black."

He pauses and looks at me. "And you're Zora's niece," he says wonderingly.

"Well," I say with shy dignity, yet with some tinge, I hope, of a nineteenth-century blush, "I'm illegitimate. That's why I never knew Aunt Zora."

I love him for the way he comes to my rescue. "You're *not* illegitimate!" he cries, his eyes resting on me fondly. "All of us are God's children. Don't you even *think* such a thing."

And I hate myself for lying to him. Still, I ask myself, would I have gotten this far toward getting the headstone and finding out about Zora Hurston's last days without telling my lie? Actually, I probably would have. But I don't like taking chances that could get me stranded in central Florida.

"Zora didn't get along with her family. I don't know why. Did you read her autobiography, *Dust Tracks on a Road*?"

"Yes, I did," I say. "It pained me to see Zora pretending to be naive and grateful about the old white 'Godmother' who helped finance her research, but I loved the part where she ran off from home after falling out with her brother's wife."

Dr. Benton nods. "When she got sick, I tried to get her to go back to her family, but she refused. There wasn't any real hatred; they just never had gotten along and Zora wouldn't go to them. She didn't want to go to the county home, either, but she had to, because she couldn't do a thing for herself."

"I was surprised to learn she died of malnutrition."

Dr. Benton seems startled. "Zora didn't die of malnutrition," he says indignantly. "Where did you get that story from? She had a stroke and she died in the welfare home." He seems peculiarly upset, distressed, but sits back reflectively in his chair. "She was an incredible woman," he muses. "Sometimes when I closed my office, I'd go by her house and just talk to her for an hour or two. She was a well-read, well-traveled woman and always had her own ideas about what was going on. . . ."

"I never knew her, you know. Only some of Carl Van Vechten's photographs and some newspaper photographs. . . . What did she look like?"

"When I knew her, in the fifties, she was a big woman, erect. Not quite as light as I am [Dr. Benton is dark beige], and about five foot, seven inches, and she weighed about two hundred pounds. Probably more. She . . ."

"What! Zora was fat! She wasn't in Van Vechten's pictures!"

"Zora loved to eat," Dr. Benton says complacently. "She could sit down with a mound of ice cream and just eat and talk till it was all gone."

While Dr. Benton is talking, I recall that the Van Vechten pictures were taken when Zora was still a young woman. In them she appears tall, tan, and healthy. In later newspaper photographs—when she was in her forties—I remembered that she seemed heavier and several shades lighter. I reasoned that the earlier photographs were taken while she was busy collecting folklore materials in the hot Florida sun.

"She had high blood pressure. Her health wasn't good . . . She used to live in one of my houses—on School Court Street. It's a block house. . . .

I don't recall the number. But my wife and I used to invite her over to the house for dinner. *She always ate well,*" he says emphatically.

"That's comforting to know," I say, wondering where Zora ate when she wasn't with the Bentons.

"Sometimes she would run out of groceries—after she got sick—and she'd call me. 'Come over here and see 'bout me,' she'd say. And I'd take her shopping and buy her groceries.

"She was always studying. Her mind—before the stroke—just worked all the time. She was always going somewhere, too. She once went to Honduras to study something. And when she died, she was working on that book about Herod the Great. She was so intelligent. And really had perfect expressions. Her English was beautiful." (I suspect this is a clever way to let me know Zora herself didn't speak in the "black English" her characters used.)

"I used to read all of her books," Dr Benton continues, "but it was a long time ago. I remember one about . . . it was called, I think, 'The Children of God' [*Their Eyes Were Watching God*], and I remember Janie and Teapot [Teacake] and the mad dog riding on the cow in that hurricane and bit old Teapot on the cheek. . . ."

I am delighted that he remembers even this much of the story, even if the names are wrong, but seeing his affection for Zora I feel I must ask him about her burial. "Did she really have a pauper's funeral?"

"She *didn't* have a pauper's funeral!" he says with great heat. "Everybody around here loved Zora."

"We just came back from ordering a headstone," I say quietly, because he is an old man and the color is coming and going on his face, "but to tell the truth, I can't be positive what I found is the grave. All I know is the spot I found was the only grave-size hole in the area."

"I remember it wasn't near the road," says Dr. Benton more calmly. "Some other lady came by here and we went out looking for the grave and I took a long iron stick and poked all over that part of the cemetery but we didn't find anything. She took some pictures of the general area. Do the weeds still come up to your knees?"

"And beyond," I murmur. This time there isn't any doubt. Dr. Benton feels ashamed.

As he walks us to our car, he continues to talk about Zora. "She couldn't really write much near the end. She had the stroke and it left her weak; her mind was affected. She couldn't think about anything for long.

"She came here from Daytona, I think. She owned a houseboat over there. When she came here, she sold it. She lived on that money, then she worked as a maid—for an article on maids she was writing—and she worked for the *Chronicle* writing the horoscope column.

"I think black people here in Florida got mad at her because she was for some politician they were against. She said this politician built schools for blacks while the one they wanted just talked about it. And although Zora wasn't egotistical, what she thought, she thought; and generally what she thought, she said."

When we leave Dr. Benton's office, I realize I have missed my plane back home to Jackson, Mississippi. That being so, Charlotte and I decide to find the house Zora lived in before she was taken to the county welfare home to die. From among her many notes, Charlotte locates a letter of Zora's she has copied that carries the address: 1734 School Court Street. We ask several people for directions. Finally, two old gentlemen in a dusty gray Plymouth offer to lead us there. School Court Street is not paved, and the road is full of mud puddles. It is dismal and squalid, redeemed only by the brightness of the late afternoon sun. Now I can understand what a "block" house is. It *is* a house shaped like a block, for one thing, surrounded by others just like it. Some houses are blue and some are green or yellow. Zora's is light green. They are tiny—about fifty by fifty feet, squatty with flat roofs. The house Zora lived in looks worse than the others, but that is its only distinction. It also has three ragged and dirty children sitting on the steps.

"Is this where y'all live?" I ask, aiming my camera.

"No, ma'am," they say in unison, looking at me earnestly. "We live over yonder. This Miss So-and-So's house; but she in the horspital."

We chatter inconsequentially while I take more pictures. A car drives up with a young black couple in it. They scowl fiercely at Charlotte and don't look at me with friendliness, either. They get out and stand in their doorway across the street. I go up to them to explain. "Did you know Zora Hurston used to live right across from you?" I ask.

"Who?" They stare at me blankly, then become curiously attentive, as if they think I made the name up. They are both Afroed and he is somberly dashikied.

I suddenly feel frail and exhausted. "It's too long a story," I say, "but tell me something: is there anybody on this street who's lived here for more than thirteen years?"

"That old man down there," the young man says, pointing. Sure enough, there is a man sitting on his steps three houses down. He has graying hair and is very neat, but there is a weakness about him. He reminds me of Mrs. Turner's husband in *Their Eyes Were Watching God*. He's rather "vanishing"-looking, as if his features have been sanded down. In the old days, before black was beautiful, be was probably considered attractive, because he has wavy hair and light-brown skin; but now, well, light skin has ceased to be its own reward.

After the preliminaries, there is only one thing I want to know: "Tell me something," I begin, looking down at Zora's house. "Did Zora like flowers?"

He looks at me queerly. "As a matter of fact," he says looking regretfully at the bare, rough yard that surrounds her former house, "she was crazy about them. And she was a great gardener. She loved azaleas, and that running and blooming vine [morning-glories], and she really loved that night-smelling flower [gardenia]. She kept a vegetable garden year-round, too. She raised collards and tomatoes and things like that.

"Everyone in this community thought well of Miss Hurston. When she died, people all up and down this street took up a collection for her burial. We put her away nice."

"Why didn't somebody put up a headstone?"

"Well, you know, one was never requested. Her and her family didn't get along. They didn't even come to the funeral."

"And did she live down there by herself?"

"Yes, until they took her away. She lived with—just her and her companion, Sport."

My ears perk up. "Who?"

"Sport, you know, her dog. He was her only companion. He was a big brown-and-white dog."

When I walk back to the car, Charlotte is talking to the young couple on their porch. They are relaxed and smiling.

"I told them about the famous lady who used to live across the street from them," says Charlotte as we drive off. "Of course they had no idea Zora ever lived, let alone that she lived across the street. I think I'll send some of her books to them."

"That's real kind of you," I say.

> I am not tragically colored. There is no great sorrow dammed up in my soul, nor lurking behind my eyes. I do not mind at all. I do not belong to the sobbing school of Negrohood who hold that nature somehow has given them a lowdown dirty deal and whose feelings are all hurt about it. . . . No, I do not weep at the world-I am too busy sharpening my oyster knife.
>
> —Zora Neale Hurston, "How It Feels
> To Be Colored," *World Tomorrow,* 1928

There are times—and finding Zora Hurston's grave was one of them—when normal responses of grief, horror, and so on do not make sense because they bear no real relation to the depth of the emotion one feels. It was impossible for me to cry when I saw the field full of weeds where Zora is. Partly this is because I have come to know Zora through her books and she was not a teary sort of person herself; but partly, too, it is because there is a point at which even grief feels absurd. And at this point, laughter gushes up to retrieve sanity.

It is only later, when the pain is not so direct a threat to one's own existence, that what was learned in that moment of comical lunacy is understood. Such moments rob us of both youth and vanity. But perhaps they are also times when greater disciplines are born.

HOLY CITY

The ways of Sion do mourn, because none come to the solemn feasts; all her gates are desolate; her priests sigh, her virgins are afflicted, and she is in bitterness. (*The Lamentations of Jeremiah*)

He is not here: for He is risen, as he said. Come, see the place where the Lord lay. (*Matthew 28:6*)

J erusalem was not, at first, a geographic place on my map; it existed for me only as metaphor, and to think of it otherwise seemed even a little gauche, like asking for a chemical analysis of the communion wine. I had never thought of it as a place I might visit until I was offered a chance to attend an international book fair there. Even then, I hesitated. My vague sense of a "real" place called Jerusalem was infused with danger.

"Oh, but you can walk the stations of the cross!" a friend of mine said.

"I can do that here," I said, thinking of plaques nailed to the trees in the woods of a convent upstate.

"No," she said, "these are the *real* stations, where Jesus actually walked." With those words she made the spiritual Jerusalem geographical to me, and I was not at all sure that was what I wanted it to become.

Still, the thought of achieving some as-yet-unimagined depth of religious experience started to sneak in and take its hold. People started telling me about Jerusalem syndrome, in which a devout seeker actually goes mad and ends up standing outside the gates in sackcloth and ashes, calling the people to repentance, claiming to be Moses or Jeremiah or John the Baptist or Mary Magdalene. This gave me a shiver; I could imagine it happening to me. I began to set aside the books I would take with me: Augustine's *Confessions*, Bernanos's *La Joie*, Merton's *Seven Story Mountain*, which I was ashamed I hadn't yet read. I might be going for work, but I would make it a pilgrimage. These were books to read in silent spaces. I had yet to discover that silence was no feature of the holy city.

It was 1993, and the Intifada was in full swing. But I had little sense of the conflict there beyond the general American understanding that people are all a little crazy in the Middle East. At a gathering given by the organizers for the people going to the book fair, I stood in a small group of neophytes listening to a veteran prepare us for the city.

"Jerusalem is such a tremendous place for Jews," he said. "If you're Jewish it's tremendously powerful to see that city. It doesn't matter if you've never been religious before."

"Yes," I said enthusiastically, joining in the spirit, "I imagine it must be powerful for Christians too, from everything I've heard. . . . " I was thinking of "the real stations," where Jesus walked, and the penitent Mary Magdalenes at the city gate, but the Jerusalem veteran didn't seem to hear me.

"Really, for any Jew, it's an overwhelming thing; you can't help but feel the connection," he went on. When he finished, and everyone had nodded, I tried again.

"You know, as a Catholic, I'm really looking forward to. . . ." He turned his back to me. I stood there, embarrassed in the way one is when left with half a sentence hanging out and no way either to finish it or to pull it back in, wondering how it could be possible he hadn't heard me.

It had not yet occurred to me how much of life and politics is in what one hears, and what one chooses not to hear—and in the meaning one finds, the interpretation one gives, to the words that get through. It has taken me some time to begin to understand that this man might not have been talking, really, about religion in the religious sense, but about the feeling of encountering a community that wraps itself around you like a warm robe, of not being an outsider. Of finding that the calendar is your calendar, that the holidays are your holidays, not someone else's. Of feeling that the powers that be are already on your side (rather than against you) because of a shared tradition, that no one who matters is making assumptions that exclude you. Few Jews, I imagine, are raised with the luxury of thinking of Jerusalem "only" as metaphor. For me to interject into such a discussion my vision of Jerusalem as transcendent, holy to all faiths, was a big boo-boo; perhaps my back-turning colleague was only trying to spare me the acknowledgment of this. Or perhaps he simply did not want to explain what he felt to an outsider.

At the same time I thought I could relate to what he was saying. I'd been casting about for a while for some clue as to what it meant to be Catholic, some sense of being part of a living tradition. I was open to the possibility that Jerusalem could tie us all closer to our faiths—Why not?

I was completely unprepared for the physical and political nature of the place, the smell of orange blossoms and dry heat when I left the airport in Tel Aviv. I was shocked to see, on the outside wall of a religious school, a sign with an American flag thanking "the people of the United States" for support in building it—wasn't it illegal to use government funds to build religious schools in our own country? I was astonished to see teenaged kids everywhere, sauntering and chatting and drinking Coca-Cola, as one might expect, gorgeous tresses of long black curls trailing down the backs of many of the girls—but in uniform and with machine guns casually slung under their arms or across their backs.

We arrived, without knowing it, on Good Friday for Eastern Orthodox Christians. (Easter Sunday was also Holocaust Memorial Day, an impossible conjunction for someone who might want to recognize both.) The following night, a British journalist led a small group of us to dinner in East Jerusalem, at an old hotel "known" to be a "secret" meeting place of diplomats and the PLO: The American Colony, an exotic place richly decorated with carpets and tiles, with a courtyard of lemon and orange trees. (Our British companions, with their national memory of having once owned the place, didn't shy away from the Arab quarters as many of the Americans did.) In the balmy courtyard we drank excellent wine from Galilea, and inside we ate from dozens of delicious tiny dishes, plates appearing and disappearing at the hands of four gracious waiters—British colonialism suddenly understandable as quite a good idea, from the colonial point of view. But having discovered the Eastern Orthodox calendar, I was determined to find a way to the midnight Easter vigil at the Church of the Holy Sepulcher, the holiest place in Christendom, deep in the Muslim quarter of the Old City. I was afraid to go alone, so the only option was to persuade my dinner companions—a group from many backgrounds—to go with me. Our waiters pointed the way, only a short walk, they said, to the Damascus Gate.

Holy city, eternal city, city of light, whereof Jeremiah spoke, "For lo, I will call all the families of the kingdoms of the north, saith the Lord; and they shall come, and they shall set every one his throne at the entering of the gates of Jerusalem, and against all the walls thereof round about . . ."

City of stones. The feel of them, ancient and worn, under thin-soled shoes, has a charismatic effect on the whole body. In the dark, they are companions, absorbing fear, on the way from the Damascus Gate toward the Church of the Holy Sepulcher. The streets are far from empty. To the side, the shuttered market stalls reveal their presence by smell: of pepper; of hard cheese and animal blood; of cumin and coriander and especially of cardamom, a cacophony of spices; of olives and vinegar; of dusty wool and oiled new wood; of coffee and sweet hot mint tea. Some of the coffee stalls are still open to serve the crowd of people flowing from doors and arches and alleys, down stairs, some carrying candles or folding chairs or wooden stools, into the main artery toward the Church that Saint Helena, mother of Constantine, built to mark the sites she identified through legend and inner vision as those of the crucifixion and burial of Jesus.

The crowd thickens and slows. Some stalls are open to sell candles, rosary beads, holy water from the River Jordan, small vials of blessed earth from this sacred land. There is a heavy, resonating report against the stones, a striking sound of wood against rock; and again, vibrating through the crowd and parting it; and again, as the black-cloaked and mitered Greek Orthodox priest, with long gray beard stretching to his waist, lifts his gilded staff and brings it down sharply. He is at the head of a robed procession of swaying priests, all with ornate, heavy staffs, with which, every few steps, they strike the stones. There is a burst of chanting and then another, somewhere else in the dark. Inside the vast church, the crowd of hundreds mills about—Armenians, Palestinians, Greeks, Africans, women in embroidered dress and white head scarves, men smoking, hundreds holding candles, dripping hot wax, chanting, waiting. The church is cavernous. Near the empty Roman Catholic chapel, in a little-used part of the church that smells of urine, there are building materials on the floor. In the center, the Orthodox vigil is going on: all the candles are lit; small gold tasseled tapestries, hung high on staffs, twist and swing over the heads of the crowd, which chants, stops, waits, and chants again.

The smell of incense is overpowering, stinging my throat and mouth, already dry from too much Galilean red wine. Around the sides of the church, people mill about, talking. Behind the tiny shrine, which one bends to enter, built around Jesus' tomb, a group of men huddle around a prayer book, singing and chanting, while the women sit at the sides, watching, praying, resting, waiting. They are Coptics, an ancient Egyptian Christian sect. Upstairs, in a chapel hung with gold lamps around large Byzantine crucifix, someone tells me to put my hand through a gold-rimmed hole in the floor, under the altar. I do, and feel cool, smooth, flat rock. The rock of Golgotha.

I stand up and see an old woman, her face finely lined and serene, in a chair with her stockinged feet tucked under her, fast asleep. A bearded Orthodox priest is teaching something to a small boy, who is writing something on a pad; he shows it to the priest, who nods and smiles. I fret about how to cross myself and pray without being seen by my intellectual colleagues, and manage to position myself behind a pillar. Three Israeli security police saunter through in their tan uniforms, rifles slung over their shoulders.

Downstairs, old women are strewing rose petals over the marble slab representing the place of the Extreme Unction, where Jesus' body was washed before burial. The slab is wet with pools of water, which seem to have appeared miraculously, while the women kiss the stone, dampen their rosary beads in the water, and bathe and stroke their own worn faces with it, praying. It seems that the stone will be bathed eternally, that it has never been dry since Jesus' body was washed on the spot.

From another upstairs room there is a stairway to an Ethiopian monastery, an African village of mud-walled cells on the roof of the church, near the pillar marking the ninth station, where Jesus falls for the third time. Down in the courtyard, light spills from a crowded chapel of Ethiopians quietly singing, wrapped head to toe in dazzling white cloth, their smooth, dark faces radiantly beautiful in a wash of light from oil lamps and candles, the mood more solemn and still than in the main church.

The next morning, in West Jerusalem, those of us who had ventured down the Damascus Road from the orange- and lemon-scented courtyard of the American Colony Hotel into the Old City at night were roundly condemned for our foolishness. A tourist, they said, had been stabbed in an East Jerusalem street a few months before. One of my companions, recounting what he'd seen in the church, commented in awestruck tones, "You could see, right there, the source of everything that's wrong with the world, all that fanaticism."

> She weepeth sore in the night, and her tears are on her cheeks; among
> all her lovers she hath none to comfort her; all her friends have dealt
> treacherously with her; they are become her enemies.

I wonder how European medieval pilgrims felt when they reached the
Holy City after months and months of difficult, dangerous travel. Were
they disappointed to find a city made of earth and stones, like other
cities? Did the physical sites of their belief seem real, or hollow? Did
they always believe that their relics were indeed fragments of the True
Cross? Or were they conscious of the sediment put down by centuries,
layers of meaning and sensibility, on any one of which they might be al-
lowing themselves to be conned, or ridiculous? Or were they hooligans,
rowdies, adventurers along for the ride? Were they spellbound by the
landscape, its gorgeous hills spotted with white stone, its sudden shifts
in terrain from one hill to another; confused by its accretions of time
and meaning; frightened by its politics; entranced by its suggestions of
the presence of the invisible and frustrated by its invisibility, as I was?
Were they all of the above?

Jerusalem asks more questions than it answers. Its literalness, the flesh
of its existence in history—its churches with their layers of Franciscan
stucco over Ottoman embellishment of Crusader castle built on Byzantine
ruins of Herodian stone—the flesh of its existence in history is fascinating,
and embarrassing.

I met a young Jewish man who had "made aliyah" (returned to Israel
out of religious devotion) and had been living in Jerusalem. Jerusalem, he
said, was another Disneyland, a religious theme park. Living there had
made him lose his faith.

The Friday after Orthodox Easter, I followed a procession along the
Via Dolorosa, with the "real stations, where Jesus walked." The procession
was led by a young Roman priest with a microphone; the familiar chants
were overpowered by the call to prayer at the nearby Dome of the Rock,
broadcast over loudspeakers. The mass of yellow sun hats worn by a large

group of tourists trying to stay together threatened any devotional mood; many held video cameras over the heads of the crowd while brown-frocked friars, looking bored and grimly ignoring the flashbulbs, tried to herd the crowd in the right direction. The Muslims had a much better sound system, while the Franciscans had only one small amplifier, which a lead friar carried on a shoulder strap while he and his brethren read and sang into the microphone. At the third station, he read the only lines I could hear clearly: "We live in an earthly city; yet we look for a heavenly one." *No kidding,* I thought.

Then, as at each station, he led the prayers: "Our Father. Hail Mary. Glory be. The fourth station, Veronica wipes the face of our Lord."

I had seen two rooms of the Last Supper, one over a Syrian Orthodox convent with few visitors. I had also seen two sites of Jesus' burial. The Anglican one in a garden—full of cheerful Britishers photographing each other before the cave—had been established by those who dissented from Saint Helena's view, on which the Church of the Holy Sepulcher had been built. The overgrown place had its own sweet romance; it seemed more true than the gilded shrines of the Holy Sepulcher. A painted sign fixed to the gate of the Tomb reminded visitors "He *is* not here, He is risen."

At the end of the procession of the stations of the cross, I was back in the Holy Sepulcher, and after the last station, where Christ is laid in his tomb, I peered in at a Coptic priest with his yellowed beard trailing over his belly, guarding the shrine behind the tomb. He allowed me to take his picture and to kiss his cheek in thanks. He reached to the altar beside him and pressed something into my palm: a small wooden cross with a tin figure of Christ. I wasn't sure at first whether he meant me to keep it; I thought it was some ritual and I was supposed to stand there, the cross in the center of my palm, and say a prayer or perhaps a confession. The priest seemed to be waiting for me to do something, I didn't know what. Then he jostled my hand, indicating that the cross was mine to keep. It some-how seemed an answer to a question I hadn't even realized I'd asked, a communication I hadn't even known I was thirsty for, and I clutched it, overwrought with emotion. All this time, I realized, I had been waiting for some kind of sign, and this one seemed so generous and concrete that on a stone step nearby, I sat and cried. Then I went to sit and pray in a silent ancient catacomb housing Joseph of Arimathea's tomb.

When I came out again the Coptic priest was still there, his yellow beard a streak across his vestments. He brought an extra stool into his shrine and made me sit beside him, while we tried to communicate in his very few words of English and my even fewer words of Arabic. He seemed delighted at my company, apologetic that he didn't have more English words to share with me, that the words he had were like unruly marbles in his snaggle-toothed mouth. He pressed two more crosses into my hand from a box by his side that I hadn't seen before—along with candles, intended to be given in return for donations. That had been what he had been waiting for before, but now that he'd seen the impression the cheap little cross had made on me, he wanted me to have more, *gratis*. I think he might have showered me with crosses if I'd wanted. He smiled hugely in his beard.

If the first cross had seemed a sign, the other two seemed a divine wink of uncertain meaning, both joke and affirmation. I clutched them in my sweaty hand. Three crosses, like the three lighted ones I had seen from a train from Washington a few months before, after an intense weekend with two friends in which deep discussion of Catholicism had alternated with sweaty dancing in gay discos. Kitsch, like the three homemade triptychs of the Virgin Mary my friend P. had found at a yard sale and divided up among the three of us. Now I had three cheap wood and tin souvenirs, or signs of grace, to be divided the same way. I had spent much of my time in the Holy City wishing my friends were there, to witness and grapple its strange alloys of sacred and secular. Three months after my return from Jerusalem, both would test positive for HIV; one would live, one would die.

I took the three crosses to dip them in the water on top of the marble slab of the Extreme Unction, as I had seen the old Greek women do. But the slab was by now almost entirely dry, scattered with withered rose petals, and I could rub them in only a few remaining spots of dampness.

CLIMBING TO CHRISTMAS

I t is the day after Christmas and I am back in St. Luke's Hospital on the porch at Scrymser, floor seven, staring east into a roiled red and purple morning sky. Once more in that place where two years and nine months ago, March of 1984, I died and was born again: a place I had hoped never to revisit. The crevasses of Harlem are still lit in that partial way with an illuminated grid or two above a few dark towers and a flake of light—a plane rising from or drifting down into La Guardia and off to the left a sheet of gray water.

Yesterday morning I was in the hospital chapel. There on the balcony, a handful of us were weakly singing the Christmas hymns: "Hark! the Herald Angels," "Adeste Fideles," "O Little Town of Bethlehem," "Silent Night."

Then the service was over, the chaplain and organist were gone, and we waited in our hospital gowns and paper slippers for our caretakers to come and wheel or lead us away: an old lady, another old gentleman besides myself, two worn-looking younger women, and a couple in street clothes waiting for news, good or bad. Someone began to sing "The First

Noel." We all joined in a cappella, thin and wobbly, but on key and maybe just a bit defiant. For me there was a sort of cumulative miracle, unexpected yet emphatic, a shining package with the words embedded in it.

This was the same hymn that, three months ago, I was singing in the manger at Bethlehem. There were sixteen of us, students enrolled in the long course, "The Bible and the Holy Land, Home of Three Great Faiths," at St. George's College in Jerusalem. Fifteen were hale, strong-lunged, young Third World clergymen of many denominations from many places: Taiwan, Brazil, Hong Kong, India, Tahiti, Cebu, Zimbabwe. And then there was me, the ringer, recently retired from the Columbia School of Journalism and pushing seventy, and who was barely an Episcopalian. With the manger all to ourselves, and with Christmas still a season away, we sang.

Here is the sort of thing that had been going on all fall in a land where miracles were commonplace: a climb up Tabor, the Mount of Transfiguration; Masada (the funicular down, not up); up both ends of Carmel; Scopus, many times; Ein Gedi; the Herodium; a thousand steps up the Mount of Temptation (with my defective heart what was I thinking of?); up the slow slope of the Mount of the Beatitudes, looking the heart-breaking, miracle-strewn distance down over Capernaum, over Tabgha to the Sea of Galilee. Up to Belvoir, up the Mount of Olives—not, however, the seven thousand steps up Sinai, but instead looking up in awe from St. Catherine's, the site of the Burning Bush, to the red stone heap above.

Still, a lot of climbing. A pilgrim (I was after all a pilgrim) is expected to climb and visit—a lot of visits—to caves, to tunnels and tombs, to churches and palaces, tels and crypts, to Joshua's Jericho, John's Jordan, digs and open fields, Megiddo where (at the moment it seems quite likely) the final battle is to be fought, Nazareth, Cana (water into wine), Acco, Nebi Samwil, Lod, Safed, San Saaba, Gamala, Gadara (the maddened swine), Emmaus (the resurrection confirmed). The Judean wilderness, pink and mauve, spread out before me with Bethany (the raising of Lazarus), Gethsemane, the Mosque of Omar, the Temple Wall, Calvary and the Sepulcher somewhere at my back. Spots holy and not so—Sodom to the right as we rattle south past Qumran to Akaba—and everywhere a conviction of authenticity, that this is certainly where it all happened—the history, the prodigies, the miracles.

Now, the Holy Land behind me, it is as if the nurses' aide had put me in my chair with wheels, a blanket across my lap, and intentionally pushed me through all those bleak hospital corridors to a final bright eminence.

Those men in their green dusters with their masks, their bakers' hats, their knives and saws—I have survived them. It is a miracle reinforced, realized, riding on top of our thin, wispy patients' voices.

Nor is it so dire as all this obliquity would seem to suggest, to be back in the hospital, recovering, they assured me (and I don't doubt it, as they have been right before with two heart attacks and one excised cancer), from a quintuple bypass. Not dire at all, but quite homey. There was a long wait for surgery from Friday noon to early evening, the last Friday but one of Advent, and the last bypass of the week, with my wife Mary Ellin and our youngest daughter Katherine filling the time singing, not the appropriate carols, but all the songs we sang on the long drive to the beach, from the country into the city, or to Des Moines—the six of us, four children and two grownups, in our tarnished gold Chrysler station wagon with the defective shock absorbers, singing "Blue Skies," "Don't Bring Lulu," "Let's Have Another Cup of Coffee," "Mean to Me"—until they finally wheeled me away on a gurney with creaking wheels and a thin blanket up to my chin, not all that scared, a molehill being pushed to Mohammed.

Later, Mary Ellin and the three clergymen given the right to visit in the recovery room said I looked appalling, that I had as many tubes and wires hanging from me as a cuttlefish has tentacles, not a particularly pretty picture. And when they asked me how I felt, how it felt, I gave them all a very cold look and said, as Mary Ellin reports, "Disagreeable," answering both questions at once.

Now, for the moment, they are gone—the tubes and wires, the clergy-men, my wife and daughter—and across my chest is a kind of grate, as if, were it not there, my heart might escape, swell, and flap away. Yesterday at chapel and a little later it seemed it must do just that, swell and break through. But it was contained. My breath is shallow. I shuffle like the old man I have recently been claiming to be: not pretending now, but the real thing. Tubeless and wireless, I look in my lavatory mirror, and the face is gray almost as death—but death departing, not homing in.

Sometime during the eleven weeks I was in Israel, Mary Ellin had her sixtieth birthday. Katherine and Benjy gave the party, their first in their new apartment on Washington Heights, and read my greetings from the Holy Land. I celebrated our thirty-fifth anniversary in a sleeping bag on the cooling sands of the Sinai. And when I was back in Jerusalem, Mary Ellin phoned to tell me that Elizabeth, our eldest, was expecting a baby, our first grandchild, next May.

Coming up from walking Molly in Riverside Park, I had felt a little odd, short of breath, slightly dizzy: not much to go on, a ghost of older symp-toms. After climbing every mountain in the Holy Land, to succumb to a few steps up from Riverside Drive to Claremont Avenue, which was what I was doing, seemed ludicrous.

So I am back where I have been many times before. They have, I am told, split me open like a chicken, rearranged things, and sewed me back up, as good as new, or at least a lot better than I was.

Mary Ellin reports that her father called, asking, before she could tell him the latest development, to talk to me. He had just got the card I sent him from Jerusalem, and with that curiosity which at ninety-eight is still not satisfied, demanded an accounting of what was going on in the land of his forefathers. Mary Ellin gave him my current address. "Oh, my God," he said, which was, in my opinion, an appropriate response. The in-laws' flowers are conspicuous on my hospital windowsill along with a hand-made Christmas card from our artist son, and the animals from the

Christmas stocking our middle daughter put together for me: a papier-mâché zebra, a glass frog, a stuffed seal. Beyond the pane, past the largest Gothic church in Christendom, a mountain in gray stone, are the pigeons, the peacocks, and the chickens, in the sun of the cathedral yard.

Temper the wind to the shorn lamb—where do the old enter into that prescription? Are the old shorn, or are they covered by the wool of experience? Are the bright-eyed and bushy-tailed young (certainly not a shorn image) the truly shorn, having not yet grown their winter coats? It is another of those sayings that flips under examination, and then flips again. Did this latest sickness, did my sojourn in the Holy Land, shear me or furnish me with another, thicker blanket? And is it more desirable, after all, to be shorn—better to be exposed than protected?

Indeed, at sixty-six, should I have been camping out in the Sinai, in the sand in a sleeping bag, celebrating a distant anniversary with questionable food and drink? Should I have been staring sleepless across a dry, stony valley to a soaring cliff that could be, under an almost full moon, a sleeping city, a deserted monastery, a derelict temple? Should I have strayed so far from the Holy Land as Wadi Natrum, across the Red Sea, across the Nile? I staggered from monastery to monastery, real ones now, no hallucinations. Across the Libyan Desert, a grim stretch of it where the Desert Fathers once sat in front of their caves weaving baskets, eating dates and unleavened bread, welcoming the occasional seeking stranger, growing old staring into the wavering distance, and me disoriented by a bilious stomach and a defective inner ear, trailing a group of hearty tourists from the Netherlands who got there first.

As the group elder, I had been allowed to carry the cross into the Church of the Holy Sepulcher and read the meditation before the tomb. I had been the first to read the Scripture and designate the hymns to be sung in the red wastes of the Sinai alongside the beehive huts—"the tombs of the damned." "A jolly desert," Lawrence of Arabia told Robert Graves. The Jews thought otherwise.

At St. George's College, I was not only the oldest but also the only un-ordained student. But no one among that group of young clergymen was likely to take back to their congregations on five continents more than I, speechless, took to an unwitting congregation on that chapel balcony at St. Luke's Hospital. And it seemed to me a fair and appropriate distribution.

The list for my last day in Jerusalem:

THE DOME OF THE ROCK

THE FOUNTAIN OF SULTAN QA'IT BAY

ST. ANNE'S

THE MARMALUKE HOUSES

THE ABYSSINIAN CHAPEL

THE CHURCH OF ST. MARY MAGDALENE

THE TOMB OF THE KINGS

THE BETHESDA POOL

I got as far as the Damascus Gate, where I met a classmate, a worldly Australian destined for a lifetime in a monastery in England, who said that four Arab students had been shot by Israeli soldiers up north and the army was pouring into the Old City by the Dung Gate in expecta-tion of bad trouble. I turned back.

In the Holy Land everyone has fertile ground for anger. The old. The young. The Jews. The Arabs. When I heard the grievances of the Jews, I felt sorry for the Arabs. When I heard the Arabs, it was the Jews I felt sorry for. Facing the young, I did not know what to think.

So approaching three score and ten I have managed a peak experience. Does a pilgrimage to Jerusalem and back make me a little short of being old? Pilgrims are of no particular age. But perhaps pilgrims who come back are not yet quite old. And now with my quintuple bypass I am back yet again.

REPARATION SPOKEN HERE?

T his is how I thought it would be to travel in Poland: my image of myself, of my mother and the other family members I would meet there, was strangely irradiated. I pictured us as figures on a photographic negative—our dark hair white, our faces darkened, all of us staring with white eyes at a world that would not recognize us. On the sidewalks of Krakow we would weave mute and unseen, ghostly figures superimposed on a city oblivious to our presence.

I have yet to hear a discussion of Holocaust reparations that does not make me queasy. Terms like 'justice' taste bitter; the money and property involved seem dangerous, inviting misinterpretation by those who would believe my great-aunts and others like them are just out for gain. Certainly the most important losses are irreparable. At times I think of my mother's family as having been scattered at the detonation of an explosion. Even now that the Holocaust is sixty years past and we are dispersed across several continents, our windows rattle hard at the slightest tremor of anti-Semitism. *Rent,* my grandparents urged my parents when I was a child. *Don't buy.* The possibility of flight was a staple of my upbringing. Despite

my American passport and secure suburban childhood, I grew up knowing all I had could be swept away. Discovering as a child that I wanted to
be a writer, I was irrationally uncomfortable with the realization that my
career would be language-bound: What if I had to move to another country, another culture? Shouldn't I be developing skills more easily trans-
plantable?

This trip to Poland was one I'd wanted to take all my life. And so
when, a month before my twenty-ninth birthday, my mother and I coor-
dinated travel plans with seven other relatives from Israel and England,
when my relatives arranged July meetings with the Krakow-based lawyer
handling the family's reparation claim, I refused to be deterred by what felt
like a surreal scheduling coincidence. That very week would cap off years
of work: I had eight days to check over the galleys for my first novel.
Resolved not to let this obligation eclipse the journey, I bundled up the
neat uncut pages and a handful of red pencils; I packed my bag and
boarded a plane to ground zero.

I had no intention of falling in love with Krakow—a city where more
than 60,000 Jews lived before World War II and where, as of the week I
arrived, there remained only 150. I had no intention of falling in love with
a single thing about Poland. I was there to see a world I'd heard about all
my life; to keep my mother company; to visit a building. Before the war,
my great-grandparents had owned a hotel in Krynica, a small spa town on
what was then the Polish-Czechoslovakian border. In 1939, when a small
knot of my family members escaped to the east, the Germans were ru-
mored to have made the hotel into barracks for Nazi soldiers. In 1949, at
the start of the communist era, the Polish government turned the building
into a high school. And in 1990, my great-aunts filed a claim on that property, as well as on the family's homes in Krakow: a claim that, by the time
eight of us converged on Krakow this June, seemed to have been buffeted
by every legal obstacle the Polish courts could muster.

There is logic to setting obstacles in the path of reparations claims—
one does not have to search hard for a motive. Most survivors are in their

eighties and nineties; my youngest great-aunt just turned seventy-five. My mother, raised by refugee parents in New York City, speaks the Polish of a five-year-old: the age at which she learned English. In a few years, there will be no one left who cares enough to do the legwork involved in pursuing the claim—no one left who ever spent a night in a room of the hotel, no one left who can decipher the legalistic Polish of the necessary documents. It seems abundantly clear that the Poles are waiting for my relatives, their memories, their Polish fluency, to die.

As soon as we boarded the plane, I asked my mother to teach me Polish. I knew the trip would be hard on her; she'd never been to her parents' homeland, though they had raised her on a diet of Polish history and European sensibilities. Not one known member of my family remains among the aging Jews of Poland—those who failed to escape to the east in 1939 did not survive. I would be the youngest of our group: the "third-generation survivor," as someone would label me, jarringly, that week. The oldest, at eighty-four, had not been back to Poland since before the war. *Jeden, dwa, trzy, cztery.* By the time we landed I'd learned to count to four; my pronunciation, as I'd hoped, kept my mother laughing. I rubber-banded the galleys—I'd made some progress during the flight—and together we stepped into the airport.

I had no intention of falling in love with Poland. But this is what happened when my mother and I reached Krakow: Boisterous Israeli relatives greeted us at the terminal. They led us into the wide streets of the city. And here, in this country I'd never visited, I turned every corner to find a familiar scene. "This is where your grandfather grew up," an aunt would tell me, and I would think: *Yes, I knew the building would be on that side of the street.* Homelands, I quickly discovered, can be hereditary. Through story upon story of my grandparents' vanished world, the blueprint of this city had been inscribed in my mind.

While two of my relatives met with the reparations lawyer, the rest of us explored the city. The degree of déjà vu I felt was unsettling. Every place we went, every window, every doorway of the old Jewish neighborhood seemed to represent a long-ago cousin. At dinner that first night, I sat with my assembled family and listened to conversations that ricocheted among Polish, English, and Hebrew, often within one sentence. To say we weren't mute is an understatement. One aunt chatted with her son in Tel Aviv via cellular phone; another stretched over a fleet of dinner plates to check whether the flowers on the table's centerpiece were real. My mother accidentally answered a Polish waiter's query in Hebrew and then, stumbling in a Polish dredged from childhood, requested ice cream rather than ice in her water. Everyone laughed. My relatives had never seemed as colorful, as individual.

The feeling was so strong it took me by surprise: *we belonged here.*

For three days, I lived in a vibrant Jewish family in Krakow. For three seductive, merciful days, Krakow was ours. Felek, my grandmother's high school boyfriend—now eighty-five—took us to a centuries-old café and sat us at the same corner table where he and my grandmother broke up one afternoon in the 1930s. *I was young. I was not good to her.* Tears gathered in Felek's eyes as he described their argument, decades before my grandmother's illness and death. *She cried so hard I didn't know what to do.* He walked us by the club where they used to dance every Tuesday afternoon. ("The usual dances. Foxtrot. Tango.") We sat in outdoor cafés on streets lined with pastel-colored buildings. We walked along the river, admired the Wawel castle. Sipping soda alone one morning at an umbrella-shaded table, I felt a hand on my shoulder. Felek, in the square for a business meeting, had spotted me. There is little for which one feels more grateful than to be recognized in a strange city.

Without a heartbeat's hesitation, I chose to let it happen. Shedding the armor of prescience with which we approach pre-Holocaust Europe, I allowed the thought: *if I forget about the anti-Semitism, I can feel at home here.* Knowingly—eagerly, even—I dropped the leaden weight of caution and boarded a train that I knew could lead only to betrayal. I let myself be enchanted by the city. It was an act of love for my grandparents, both Polish patriots in their youth, neither of whom had lived to make this family trip.

History is patronizing toward those who lived it; I chose, for these few days, to ignore history and to see Poland through their youthful eyes.

My Israeli relatives shopped; my mother and I attended a concert. We visited my grandmother's high school. Waiting for the tour to begin at the university where my grandfather fought anti-Semitic regulations, I sat on stone steps and continued work on my galleys. I looked at the pages in my hands, and for the first time ever I did not feel privately like a freak for writing this novel, set in modern Israel but narrated in part by a Polish Holocaust survivor. For once I didn't feel the need to apologize for being serious, for caring about something out of synch with my own generation. I had been drawn to this material not because I was somehow morbid but rather because this place, its politics and priorities and sensibilities, had been alive for me as long as I could remember. Here, in a country I had never expected to feel like home, I recognized myself.

We admired the woodwork of a famous church altar, videotaped the trumpet player at the top of the Mariacki Church. Mapping out an extinct family life, we visited those Krakow homes my great-aunts are trying to reclaim, and those that were so badly trashed when the Nazis crammed hundreds of families into this section of the city (the ghetto depicted in *Schindler's List,* now low-rent housing) that my aunts have chosen not to claim them. We photographed stairwells, graffiti, a rusted motorcycle covered by a tarp. Dirty kittens poked their heads out of dumpsters, dogs barked from balconies as we approached. The buildings' residents looked on with folded arms.

Certain kinds of love exact a price. It wasn't until a loud noise sent me jumping or tears surprised me during a cab ride that I had any indication of the stress beneath the surface of those days. A celebratory gun salute at a parade in Krakow's main square sent hundreds of pigeons wheeling into the air. As the beating of wings subsided I watched them settle on rooftops and wondered, heart still racing, how high the birds flew in the 1940s.

By now I knew a few Polish phrases, enough to construct a sentence here and there. I made increasingly bold forays into the language. "*Ja nie jestem kapusta!*" I am not a cabbage. By now I could count to six. If I kept this up, I realized one afternoon—if I kept this up, and the aged kept dying—I'd be able to count the remaining Jews of Krakow.

On the last night before the Israeli and British contingents of my family would depart, we sat for hours over dinner. Felek serenaded one of my Polish relatives in German: *I still remember that day . . . when the player piano played . . . that was when you first said you loved me.* The two of them ordered vodka, then beer. They hunkered down at the end of the table, speaking Polish. The rest of us watched rapt, as if their reunion in this city of their youth were a holy rite.

And then my relatives were gone. For half a week I'd lived a rich Jewish family life in a Krakow that no longer existed, an invisible city as tempting and ephemeral as one of Calvino's. Now, silences felt haunted. I practiced counting to ten. There were 149 Jews left in Krakow. One had died. The square was full of pigeons.

Things did not look good for my great-aunts' claim, according to the lawyer. Another few months and he would know more. Maybe.

The countryside en route to the Tatra Mountains was so picturesque it felt absurd. The next day my mother and I were to leave Poland; now, after a week in the city, we passed white goats on green grass, spotted cows on green grass, old men on bicycles. We passed round haystacks, rolling hills, people hand-raking hay in the fields. Even the puddles along the train tracks had ducks in them.

It took all morning to reach Krynica, a small and pretty town in the foothills of the Tatra Mountains. We made our way down streets lined with arched lampposts and tourist shops.

My great-grandparents' hotel was an imposing, run-down gray building. The broken outdoor basketball hoop and the graffiti announced the high school's long tenancy as clearly as the signs over the offices that had been my family's private rooms. You could see that it had once been beautiful. Small balconies dotted the side of the building.

It would be easy to speak of my great-grandparents' hotel as being of symbolic value to my family; after all, it has been decades since any of us resided in Poland or frequented the Tatra Mountains. But I think of a symbol as something that takes up residence in the mind. When I stood outside my great-grandparents' hotel, the building's impact was purely visceral. This was the place where my grandmother and great-aunts had vacationed; where my great-grandmother, whom I knew, presided over the family in her ultra-dignified fashion, switching into various Romance languages from time to time lest the maids be eavesdropping. In this town my grandmother swam and hiked her way into her twenties, when she defied convention and went to law school; here she skied, reluctantly, with a suitor eleven years her senior. That suitor broke a leg on the slope, and my grandmother took care of him in the hotel while he recovered. To my older relatives, the hotel is home: the inheritance their parents wanted them to have. To me it is the place where my grandparents fell in love. I wanted to see it, touch the curtains, look out at the world through those windows.

A man stepped out of a door, stared at us for a moment, then—with what seemed to be a warning look—stepped back inside.

We circled the property, took pictures. Passersby slowed to watch us. By this time we knew the routine.

But as we stood in front of the building, something unexpected happened. Normally my mother is the one to push ahead. I am the nervous Nelly, the voice of caution. Yet now I told my mother I wanted to try to go into the building, and my mother, as though sensing some nameless threat, did not want to budge. I don't know if I've ever seen her so meek.

I can't say whether it was some wordless threat radiating from the ground that stopped us, or whether we feared actual violence from those in the building. I can only say that it happened as swiftly as a blow: our personalities, our individual quirks, were swept away. Under the watchful eyes of strangers, we were no longer Anna and Rachel, grand-daughter and great-granddaughter of David and Miriam Herzig. We were simply Jews, one and two generations removed from catastrophe. And so we responded as if reading from a script, taking on our roles with astonishing ease. My mother, born on the run to refugee parents, suddenly knew to tread carefully. A small, helpless gesture of her hands was her only explanation: *I can't* or *I'm afraid.* And I, American-born, was sharply aware of one emotion: I was furious. I had a right to be here, and I believed, for just a moment, that nothing in this damn country could intimidate me. For that instant, before common sense asserted itself, I was angry enough for two—because I was an American and could afford to be.

I didn't push her to approach the building's custodians. And much as I chafed to march in and declare myself at home, I knew no combination of Polish words likely to elicit help from the strangers holding the keys to this building. I knew, too, that my grandparents and great-grandparents, with lifetimes' vocabularies at their fingertips, had received little sympathy from their countrymen. I stood on the cracked pavement, armed with little but a pocketful of numbers: evidence of all I could not express. My mother, her own vocabulary as useless as mine, stood mute beside me.

It was a sunny afternoon, an unpopular time for travel; on the Krakow-bound train the compartment, meant for six, was empty. For hours we might have been the train's only passengers. My mother and I took turns reading aloud, checking galleys against original manuscript, page after page. In our alternating voices the words sounded reassuring. Then we stopped; I continued scanning the pages by myself. The silence was eerie, interrupted only by a rhythmic thumping from the tracks.

During that train ride I stumbled, numb and exhausted, across the first way of thinking about reparations that made sense to me. The words before me were a tender language, a language for those willing to listen. But in a country where people have been reduced to artifacts, ashes, statistics—where our words are ignored or silenced and those who benefit from the murder of the Jews maintain a thick denial—only a more strident language penetrates. Reparation is a vocabulary of its own, each transaction a crude syllable sounding into a void. It forces hearing, where all else fails, on those who would rather be deaf. On that train ride I still didn't know what to feel about the political consequences of reparations, or the moral complexities. I didn't know, either, that my family's reparations claim would continue to be deadlocked, that the ensuing months of effort would produce nothing but frustration. I knew only that, for the first time ever, I was unambivalent about the reason to pursue my family's claim. I wanted my great-aunts heard.

I tried to quell the irrational notion that my mother and I were the only two passengers on a driverless train. I tried to focus on the pages in front of me. So it was my mother who saw the graffiti painted on a barrel by the railroad tracks: *Juden Raus.* "Jews Out." I looked up in time to see only freight cars: windowless bolted metal, heavy barred doors. In the picture my mother took as we passed through that anonymous country train yard, a brown hulking car fills the frame of the camera. Faintly superimposed on it is the ghostly image of a young woman—plaintive, pale, shocked Jewish features. Even now it takes me a moment to recognize my own face, reflected in the window of our compartment as my mother released the camera's shutter.

THE ROAD TO EMEI SHAN

W e spent the night at a hotel catering to Chinese tourists going up the mountain. My translator, Zha Yu, who preferred her adopted American name of Vivian, was young and efficient, bright and well traveled. The daughter of a physicist, she had been allowed to travel out of the country, had seen the Louvre, and knew which films were being censored in China. Her regular job at Chengdu television studio was not so busy that she couldn't moonlight as a translator. She had read the poems of Meng Chiao, Li Ho, Su T'ung Po, and Tu Fu, and knew a little about Buddhism, though she thought it odd that I wanted to climb all the way up a sacred mountain when I could have been driven.

The Chinese phrase for "going on a pilgrimage," *ch'ao-shan chin-hsiang*, actually means "paying one's respects to the mountain," as if the mountain were an empress or an ancestor before whom one must kneel. In China, sacred travel and the cult of the mountain were endemic. The recorded history of Taoism began during the second century A.D., and regarded mountains as home to immortals and as places where magic herbs to aid transcendence could be found. Confucians saw mountains as emblems of world order. In the Chou Dynasty beginning in 1027 B.C., imperial altars were built where emperors came to pray for prosperity. Heaven, earth, and man—the three mainstays of Chinese cosmology—were linked by the country's vertiginous peaks.

The meaning of pilgrimage changed when Taoists set up their mountain altars and Buddhist monks began plying the trails. For them pilgrimage was not only paying homage to a place of power, but also the transformation of the inner and outer environment through the physical act of walking, every step and breath altering the atmosphere, path and goal becoming the same. I thought of Mao's Long March, how step by step, year by year, his humanitarian ideals and visions of Marxist liberation were ground down to ego and tyranny.

In the evening we walked to the foot of the mountain. The main street of Emei Shan town unrolled in a single line to its base. The air was balmy and young couples walked hand in hand from shop to shop, then to a small pavilion at the top of the street where the stores stopped and the mountain began.

In ancient times the name Chu alluded not only to the region now called Sichuan, but also to the mountain, Emei Shan. Also called Lofty Eyebrows Mountain, it is traditionally thought to be the abode of the bodhisattva of pervading goodness, the protector of all those who teach the Dharma, the one who is the embodiment of essential sameness, the unifying thread that strings together all disparate things.

Across a narrow irrigation ditch that followed the road, a young, darkfaced farmer had just finished plowing his rice field. As he unharnessed his water ox, I asked if I could watch. He smiled proudly. "This is not my field or my ox but I farm it for the owners and get half the value of the crop." Forty years earlier over 25 million landlords were executed by Mao's army in an effort to purge the country of just these kinds of relationships.

I touched the neck of the ox. The wooden yoke, arched in the middle where it rested on the animal's neck, was shaped like the arched gate at the entrance to the farmstead. The farmer bade us good night and led the ox down a narrow path toward a shed.

As light left the sky, the moon rose shining in each of the flooded fields as if they were bowls and the plowed earth a roiling sea of black. Overhead a white cloud dissected trees. Was this the white mild road of early landscape paintings that led up the mountain to heaven?

"The road to Chu is hard and steep, steep as climbing to the sky!" That's what the poet Li Po once wrote. Li Po was born in Sichuan Province and honored Emei Shan as a perfect mountain that could turn him into an immortal. He probably climbed Emei Shan or at least gazed at it from afar. He also wrote, "In the West at Mount Taibo, there is a bird road that can cut across the summit of Mount Emei."

In the morning, after a breakfast of congee (a rice gruel), instant coffee, white bread, and jam, Mr. Tong drove us to the base of the mountain. The day before, when the plane had descended through clouds and smog, I knew I was dropping into a beautiful country that had been made into a living hell. Nations can be shattered, cultures can be laid on history's anvil, twisted, flattened, and decimated, but a mountain remains a mountain. Now I had to rise out of that hell on foot and I knew it would be hard.

Mr. Tong waved good-bye and said he would return in four days. Tourist buses filled the parking lot as he wove down the hill. Hefting our rucksacks onto our backs, we turned to face our pilgrim's task. Despite the stairs that were so small we had to wrench our feet sideways, it felt good to be on our way.

Shan: mountain. *Mingshan:* sacred mountain. All pilgrims stepped onto a path. The path led to a mountain. The way was crowded. From rows of rickety tables, vendors sold herbs picked on Emei Shan's slopes — ginseng, fungi, and a bundle of golden plant hairs given the shape of a dog; also amulets, walking sticks, maps, and cold spring water. Medicinal herbs seem to grow more profusely on holy mountains. No one knows why.

At a little over 6,000 feet the air was thick and humid. Women passed with baskets of strawberries and young men slung fresh-picked vegetables on their backs. Crowds of golden monkeys gathered, demanding and taking peanuts from the hands of Buddhist pilgrims and Chinese tourists. Further up the mountain an old man stepped out on the path behind me, bamboo broom in his hand, a thin long pipe in his mouth, and as I walked by, he hawked, spit, then swept my tracks clean. Trackless, I continued on.

Shu dao nan: The road to Shu is hard. There is no top, no goal. Only this hard path made of stones, the dry instruction of climbing a mountain. Every step up is a movement away from the realm of human sorrows, from the Middle Kingdom teetering between heaven and hell, from all suffering. Every step down is a slide back into it, until up and down become the same thing.

Up and up we continued, each sideways, cramped step a reminder of how difficult it is to relinquish habitual thought. "Abandon hope all ye who enter here." Dante's words had been posted above the door of the meditation hall where I sat for three and a half months in 1978. They might have said: "Welcome to the heaven or hell of your own making. Good luck climbing out." This I had already learned: If you weed the garden of your mind properly, there will be no hope and no fear, just the hard vigor of life as it plays itself out in you. But the body still resists and the mind curvets like a missile shot off and gone wild.

Emei Shan was arduous in a senseless way. I had some questions for heaven and I asked them: Why steps on a mountain path? Who carried these stones? There were stairs on the three other sacred Buddhist mountains and on the five imperial mountains and they were well used: a seventeenth-century record showed that six hundred thousand pilgrims had climbed Mount Tai. Does climbing a mountain teach about transforming effort to effortlessness? Are the two really the same, or was I a fool, were we all fools to do these things? Poor fool that I am, and often grinning through streams of sweat, I clambered on.

Every sacred mountain has its founding story. A monk or layman has a vision of a certain site and of the bodhisattva who inhabits the places. I don't know what atlas guides him, points his feet, or how he knows where to scuffle away the dirt and uncover the thin spot, the umbilicus of the mountain where its divinity is finally exposed, but it happens.

Emei Shan was opened by a man named Pu Gong. One day he was gathering some herbs on the mountain and began following deer tracks. These led him to the top of the mountain, then disappeared. Suddenly Pu Gong heard music. When he looked up he saw humans, some on horse-back, drifting toward the summit on clouds. But one figure was riding a six-tusked albino elephant and above his head glowed a halo of colored light. Pu Gong was so moved by this vision that he took off and walked all the way to India—a journey that took three months—and visited a Buddhist monk to tell him his tale. The monk listened, nodded, then passed the story on to his teacher, who interpreted Pu Gong's tale as the coming of the Bodhisattva Samantabhadra to the mountain. Pu Gong was instructed to return to Emei Shan and build a temple. Called "First Audience Hall," it was burned down by Mao's Red Guard and has since been reconstructed.

In the first century, the poet Fan Zhen wrote this quatrain:

We move to Mount Emei's highest peak;
Who knows how many thousands of layers of crags and cliffs?
A mountain monk smiles as he tells the story of Master Pu:
It was here that the white deer once left its tracks.

The further up we went, the fewer people we saw. The climate felt trop-ical, not alpine; I was bathed in sweat and the skies revealed nothing, no glimpses of high peaks. Vivian said she was too young to know much of what went on during Liberation—except that her physicist father and artist mother were put in labor reform camps where they were "struggled against." How ironic that the word liberation used by Mao was the same word used by American Buddhists to mean deliverance from samsara—human suffering—through practice. Once, going to these mountains was sanctuary, a distant retreat, a nostalgic home, a land where immortals picked herbs to prolong life, where hopping shamanic dances were danced and questions of heaven were posed. I wondered if, after the tyrannies of Mao and the Cultural Revolution, a culture could come back into being, if the human spirit could be stirred? When I asked Vivian, she said she was too young to know what had been lost and didn't see that there was a problem.

Sweating and listless, I began coughing. Having come from Hong Kong with a cold, my chest had tightened. This wasn't even a mountain by Tibetan standards, only the foothills of the Himalayas. I had walked in many mountains but nothing resembled Emei Shan: so many stairs, so many people. It was hard to see where I was, to frame the scape. Was this the axis mundi from which the spirit soared? Were the stairs the rungs of the metaphorical ladder on which Shamans climbed and the mind scratched a hole to see through?

Hogars, the young men who carried people up the mountain on narrow, slung-seated palanquins, hounded us. "Please let us carry you," they beseeched. "Bu, bu, bu, bu." No thanks, I said, and told Vivian I was shocked at the idea. "But humans carrying humans has had a long history in China," Vivian exclaimed. "It's perfectly natural."

Tea shops, temples, pavilions, and pagodas dotted the mountain. We stopped often to rest and drink cool Emei Shan spring water. At Elegant Sound Pavilion, a tumbling cataract sounded like rolling thunder. Ox Heart Pavilion was flanked on either side by the stream, which was split again by Ox Heart Rock. Golden frogs croaked and the shade of ancient nanmu trees cooled us. A Ming dynasty monk, Hong Ji, planted 69,707 of these trees, chanting a sutra and prostrating after each one went into the ground. In this way, he kept count. With only a few remaining, their shade in hot Sichuan sun still soothes tired pilgrims.

I stepped and counted. One stair equaled one of Hong Ji's trees. Rounding a bend, I entered the cool breeze of a narrow ravine called "A Strip of Heaven Cleavage." Did the rhododendrons that flowered on those steep cliffs have to climb the stairs to flower there?

Every step seemed to provoke in me more speculation. But the Chinese are still afraid to give the wrong answer. We passed a skinny porter sound asleep on his palanquin by the side of the path. A friend who had climbed Emei Shan in 1984 said the hogars had passed her on the mountain carrying a dead woman. They had wrapped her up and laid her on the sling as if she were sleeping. When my friend asked if the woman was dead the hogars said, "She's not dead, she's just very, very tired."

I asked Vivian about the mountain's geology. Was it wind or glaciers that carved these cliffs? "The gods cut through the mountains with their swords," she replied laughing. "That's the story Chinese people love to tell. Of course, I don't believe in such things."

PROVIDENCE HILL

H enry Thoreau says in his essay "Walking" that in every town there are a few old discontinued roads that may lead to profit, by which he meant adventure. Thoreau favored cross-lot walking—in other words, trespassing. He abhorred fences, boundaries, and horses—he was his own horse, as he said. He claims that to walk out into wild nature is to join with the prophets, poets, and explorers of old, the great metaphorical wanderers of history—Moses, Chaucer, Columbus, and Americus Vespucius. It is here, he wrote, on the local abandoned roads and in the unfenced woodlots and pastures that you will discover the mythologies that are the truer histories of America.

That may be. But we three are finding that the untrodden paths do not offer contemplative strolls. As soon as we approach the road, Kata's wool sweater becomes entangled and she stops and begins picking out the briars. Barkley, whose neotechnic armor sheds the spears and lances of thorny plants, turns suddenly in midtangle, his binoculars half raised, and pleads for silence.

"Listen," he says, "blackpolls. What's this? October tenth? They're right on schedule."

Here and there in the high trees we hear a lisping whistle and we can see forms darting about. We back out of the brambles and stand at the edge of the woods and the fields surrounding the farmhouse. Barkley stares at the treetops for a minute and then, without ceremony, hands the glasses to Kata, who, after much fiddling and searching, fails to see the birds and hands the glasses back. "I saw their flight," she says, "It was enough. It's what birds do."

I take the binoculars and see the small black and white forms darting among the green leaves. This is the time of their seasonal passage, the great nomadic cycle that they follow twice a year. Blackpoll warblers nest in the coniferous forests of the north. Sometime in September—flying by night, resting and feeding by day—they begin a long journey south through New England, the Central States, the American South, and then across the Gulf of Mexico to Central America, where they spend the winter. In early April, with their ancient genetic codes firing off as yet ill-understood messages, they undertake the journey in reverse.

The great migratory passages such as these would tend to make you dismiss the existence of any biological devotion to a particular place, but in fact passerine birds such as the blackpolls return year after year to the same small territories, each bird recognizing a space no larger than a few acres in a vast wildness of thousands of square miles of Canadian forest. Barkley says the same is true in their southern wintering grounds. Having flown south across the continent and the wide seas, individual birds seek out the exact area where they spent the winter in previous years, a phenomenon known in the trade as "winter site fidelity."

The blockade of brambles finally proves insurmountable, so we back out and climb again though a mix of oaks and pines, to a light woods in which other wanderers—hunters, no doubt—have passed. We see their spoor, as Barkley phrases it: an old Rheingold bottle, an aluminum pan, some oilcans, and an old mouse-shredded piece of plastic wrapper. Then, deeper in the woods, we come across a strange construction, something that looks like a cross between a chicken coop and a doghouse. The building has been overtaken by brambles and young birch, one of which has grown up through the foundation and then emerged from a window, seeking light. Growing around the doghouse Barkley finds a profusion of lactarius mushrooms.

We can see above us now the large brick house of a woman named Priscilla Eliot, a sprightly eighty-two-year-old who dresses in tweeds, wears steel-rim glasses, and favors sturdy walking shoes. I had met her earlier when I was out scouting this section of the world and explained our mission to her. She is an avid member of the Massachusetts Audubon Society and other local birding organizations, including a group known as the Rowley Dump Bird Club. Members, most of whom are women in their seventies or eighties, meet periodically to scour the New England landscape for interesting bird species. One of their favorite haunts is the town dump in Rowley, hence the name.

Mrs. Eliot's property is a finely manicured landscape in the 1920s style, with a combination of old copper beech trees, trimmed hemlock hedges, fir trees, and clipped lawns, interspersed with flower and vegetable beds. Just the type of place that reminds me of the old ferryboat suburb in which I grew up.

We keep to the east of her property and move through more tangle of blackberries and poison ivy just at the edge of an apple orchard and soon come upon the back of an old, seemingly abandoned, single-car garage set alone at the edge of the orchard. Barkley peers into a cobwebbed window, cupping his hands against the glare.

"My God," he says. "Stopped time. This is right out of Dickens. Miss Havisham's wedding day."

Inside we can see, in the half-light, dusty scythes and hay rakes, a horse-drawn sleigh, a fine leather-seated carriage, a farm wagon painted up like a Gypsy cart, and a beige 1931 Model A Ford convertible with a louvered bonnet.

As we peer in the window, a stocky man in heavy corduroys and a peaked tweed cap appears around the corner and politely clears his throat.

"Just passing through," Barkley says. "On our way to Concord."

"Out for a walk," I add to make things more clear; no one around here actually *walks* to Concord.

He lifts his cap, revealing a full head of curly gray hair, and introduces himself as Jack.

Actually, Barkley, Kata, and I rarely, if ever, just pass through. Stopping is part of the exploration of place and in a few minutes we are deep in conversation.

Jack is the gardener for Priscilla Eliot and he turns out to be a great raconteur. We learn from him that the whole orchard to the east of us, the land we are about to pass through, is doomed.

"Just last night," Jack explains, "they lost the battle to save this orchard. Developers got the okay to tear the place up and build houses. Won't see many more harvests from here. They're going to take it, every last tree, I'll bet."

We are standing at the edge of an old rutted orchard road that runs straight through the trees and then sinks down below the shoulder of the hill. In the far distance, framed by the trees, exactly beyond the road, I can see the outline of Blakes Hill just to the north of our intended route. It's a fine scene, right out of an old Wallace Nutting New England landscape, or an American impressionist painting. In fact the road must have been laid out by some sharp-eyed farmer to reveal the outline of the hill. But it's a doomed land, as Jack says.

"There's a great white-colored buck deer with a huge set of antlers that lives in this orchard," Jack says. "Hunters can't get him. They come here year after year looking for him. Sometimes manage to get a shot off. But he gets away every time, God bless him. Now what's to become of him?"

Jack tells us that one day last year, just before the winter solstice, Mrs. Eliot and the members of her bird club were sitting in the kitchen weaving greens for Christmas wreaths. Just at dusk one of them looked up and saw the great stag standing in the yard, staring in the lighted window at the circle of women. As they watched, he turned and bolted into the orchard.

"Just disappeared into thin air," Jack says.

It's a good story. Also an old story: crones sit in a circle by the hearth weaving circlets of greens from the sacred tree when a white stag appears in the gloaming out of a doomed land. Throughout the ancient world the crone was associated with witchcraft and knowledge of earth lore. The evergreen bough was sacred, the circle, even more sacred, a symbol of the eternal cycles of life and death, and the hearth was the heart of the home, the core of what the Germans call *Heimat,* a combination of home and place. The stag, by contrast, was considered the protector of wild places, the guardian, and the messenger between the wilderness and civilization. He appears in ancient India in the form of a horned god, a pre-Shiva deity. He is found in Greek mythology, as the companion of Artemis, the goddess of the hunt. He appears in Celtic mythology as Cornnums, the stag man. By the time Christianity arrived in Europe the stag had evolved into the companion of saints and crusaders. A mystic white stag guided Charlemagne through the Alps during his campaign to save Rome from barbarians. By the Middle Ages in Europe, the deer had become the symbol of more Christian saints than any other wild beast. In one popular medieval story, the pagan hunter Eustace came upon a great white stag in the forest and drew back his arrow to slay it, when a cross appeared between the stag's antlers. "I am the Redeemer," the stag said to Eustace. "Whyfore dost thou persecute me?" Eustace fell to his knees and converted on the spot. Later he was made patron saint of hunters.

Kata has spent enough time among indigenous peoples to have learned that the great mysteries of life are often revealed in daily events. Some of these incidents evolve into myth, and the place where they occurred is enshrined. Among the Native Americans she knows, who eat fast food, smoke cigarettes, and watch a lot of television, everyday events create stories that are carried on from generation to generation—an unexplained car wreck, a murder, a ghost sighting, the appearance of a black dog with red eyes, even personal memories, come to be associated with certain sections of the landscape which then become a part of the story. Nothing plays out in an empty room, stories create landscape—or vice versa: the land begets the story. Mecca was a holy spring a thousand years before Mohammed got there. Lourdes was a well-known grotto above a river on the pilgrim's way to Santiago de Compostela before Bernadette saw the Virgin there. Gay Head cliffs on Martha's Vineyard were deposited by the glacier eight thousand years before the Wampanoag Indians stood in awe of the place and came to believe that it was the home of their chief god, Marshope. Geography engenders mythology.

Unfortunately, here in the East, the first European chroniclers of the places that were considered sacred by the Pawtuckets, Nipmucks, and Massachusetts tribes chose not to set down a record of their identity; in fact they did their best to obliterate any evidence of what they considered devil worship and paganism.

The orchard rolls eastward; the land slopes. We hike down the clear dirt road at a good pace now, telling stories of holy mountains and sacred stags.

"A friend of mine in Acoma says he saw a deer leap out of the clouds," Kata says. "It appeared in the same quarter where the Indians saw Santiago come down out of the sky with a fiery sword during the Spanish siege of the town. The Spanish never could understand why the Indians surrendered; they had broken the Spanish siege when suddenly all the Indians fell back in terror. Later they told the Spanish they saw a huge knight emerge from a thunderhead on a white horse. 'That was Santiago' the Spanish explained. 'We didn't even know he was fighting with us that day.'"

"Well what about poor Actaeon?" Barkley says. "All he did was happen upon Artemis while she was bathing. She looks around for her spear and since she can't reach it, splashes water on him, and the next thing, he's got these horns. Then his own dogs chase him and he can't even call them off because now he's a full-blown stag, so the dogs down him, and along comes one of his fellow hunters and delivers the coup de grace."

"Mortals shouldn't try to look at God," Kata says.

I tell them about my brother's adventure with a fawn. He and I were hiking in the Shell Canyon in Wyoming, and at one point he went on by himself, up to a clearing in a small green valley. He was resting there when he heard a scrambling in the brush, and a fawn, drenched in perspiration, dashed out of the cover, ran up to him and stood next to him, its body touching his legs. Before he could even react, a huge "wolf" (no doubt a big coyote) charged out of the brush and, without breaking stride, ran past them and disappeared.

"Ah-ha," Kata says, "the Pawnee would say your brother's got *maxpé*, spirit power. If he believed in any of this he'd take the deer as his totem animal and wear horns. He'd go to the big Pawnee deer dances they hold. Maybe he'd even be able to see the deer woman; they say she still shows up from time to time. Dancers saw her at a big pow-wow back in 1975, a normal-looking woman, but if you look down below her skirts you see that she's got these hoofs. She seduces men and then tramples them. Some guys followed her out of the stadium the last time she showed up and they found their bodies out in the scrub, all bloodied up and trampled."

I like the image of my brother, who favors conservative, boring clothes, dressed in antlers and a loin cloth.

"You think this deer woman would trample my innocent brother? He's a social worker."

"Probably not, if he's got *maxpé.*"

Halfway down the hill we begin to hear a vast roaring, as if we are coming upon a waterfall. It's the sound of Route 495, a major north-south highway that encircles Boston, beyond the inner circle of Route 128. These great ring roads are exciting, active places, charged with angry traffic, steel and glass, and attempted landscaping. Barkley sees them as modern versions of Dante's nine circles of Hell, each designed to torture the greedy consumers in its own way. Route 495 is attempting to grow an edge city of its own about twenty-five miles south of here, at the junction with the Massachusetts Turnpike in Westborough. The two highways cut through Cedar Swamp, which was the outpost of one of the last pure-blooded Indian families in this part of the world. On cold winter days in the 1920s, they used to emerge from the swamp and beg milk from the local farmers. The swamp is also the headwaters for the Sudbury and Concord rivers, which were critical players in the American literature of landscape, the metaphorical hunting grounds for Thoreau, Emerson, and Hawthorne. The Sudbury meets the Assabet at Egg Rock in Concord, at the place the local tribes called Nawshatuck, a spot some believe was an important seasonal and ceremonial gathering site.

In our time the Sudbury and Concord are experiencing a spiritual renaissance. Several books about the rivers have been published in recent years; naturalists are taking a renewed interest in the waters; there is a national wildlife refuge strung along the river meadows; the photographer Frank Gohlke, who had worked mostly in the emptiness of the American West and Midwest, spent four years concentrating on a single stretch of the Sudbury; and because of the efforts of local conservationists with a bioregional slant, Cree Indians from Canada come to the rivers periodically to celebrate the gathering of waters and emphasize the need for protection of the waters of the world.

Barkley, Kata, and I had been debating this Route 495 problem since breakfast—mainly how to cross it. It is the major obstacle we will encounter on our walk: protected in some areas by high chain-link fences, sunk beneath deep barriers of earth in others, surrounded by concrete, and of course running with dangerous, speeding traffic. Even now, beyond the trees of the orchard, we can hear the high pitch of whining semitractor trailers charging north and south to points unknown.

After a few minutes, we break out onto an embankment above the highway and see the racing line of cars and trucks. Rush hour is coming to an end, but the tide is still running full. In fact, like all epic heroes, we have come to the traditional clashing rocks—immense, hard stone gates that roll open and then close on incautious travelers, crushing them. If the adventurous hero can get through the clashing rocks, he or she can pass beyond the restrictions of the visible world and gain access into the spirit realm or, as post-Freudian interpreters suggest, voyage inward to self-exploration and discovery.

Jason and his Argonauts had to pass clashing rocks known as the Symplegades on their way to Colchis to capture the Golden Fleece, which hung in a sacred grove and was guarded by a monster. Jason had been warned to release a dove before he attempted passage, and when the heroes came to the great rocks, they slowed the vessels and let the dove go just as the rocks rolled open. The dove made it through, and the heroes laid back on the oars and managed a safe passage. Odysseus would have sailed through the same area but he had been warned of the rolling rocks, or drifters, by the sorceress Kirke and set another course to get around them.

"The Navahos have a similar story," Kata says. "The children of Changing Woman, the Hero Twins, come to rolling rocks on their trip to visit their father the Sun. Spider Woman gave the Twins feathers plucked from the sun bird to protect them as they passed through."

We have to debate, as one always does with Barkley and Kata, the merits of the various strategies for getting through these gates of rolling cars and trucks. We watch for breaks in the traffic, but although there are slower moments, no safe passages evolve—this is, after all, a six lane highway.

"We could simply command the traffic to halt," Barkley suggests.

"The Timucuan Indians of northern Florida used to whistle at rocks and sandbars to ask for safe passage," Kata adds. "Maybe we should try that."

The hero's task is to get around or through obstacles by any means possible. And so we hike north, nearly a half a mile out of our way, to the Boston Post Road, where we turn right, and through ingenious wile (a traditional characteristic of the hero) pass *underneath* the dangerous obstacle. To my knowledge, in all of mythology no one ever thought of such a cunning trick.

For a few hundred yards or so we hike along the road and then turn south through some scrubby woods just north of an industrial park named, with unfathomable orthography, "Lyberty Park." (Seventeenth-century Concordians were not great spellers, but they were never *that* bad.)

Merchants in these parts are especially keen to have us know that this region is the so-called cradle of democracy. Undemocratic developers, businessmen, sharp-eyed land sharks, pizza sellers, dry cleaners, and gift shop owners will inform you at every turn, through signage or company names, that we are in the land of liberty.

"Whose 'lie-berty' are they celebrating, I wonder?" Kata asks.

Never mind that eighteenth-century colonials lived under a different *zeitgeist*—Kata and Barkley do not accept the premise of freedom and justice for all, when women, blacks, Native Americans, the landless, and debtors were excluded. Kata, in particular, has argued that the Native Americans might have been better off if the British had won the Revolutionary War. One of the causes of the way, she believes, was the fact that the British did not want the colonials to settle in territory west of the so-called Quebec Line, which belonged to the Indians (albeit not for the sake of the Indians). The colonials wanted to move westward, and furthermore they wanted the British Army to protect them against the legitimate (or so Kata says) raids of the affronted natives of the place.

Be that as it may, we are now walking through ground that was very much a part of what is known locally as the Concord Fight, and the locals are not going to let us forget it. On this road, on the morning of April 19, 1775, 131 members of the Westford Minutemen, under the command of Colonel John Robinson, marched to Concord to "defend," in the popular phrase, the town. Whether Concord needed defending is debatable.

John Robinson, who was forty years old at the time of the fight, was born in Topsfield in 1735 and lived on the western slopes of Prospect Hill. He was born to patriotism, having married one Hulda Perley of Boxford, who was the niece of the seasoned old fighter Israel Putnam, who had been scalped during the French and Indian Wars and survived to command the forces at Bunker Hill.

Sometime around two in the morning on April 19, 1775, Doctor Samuel Prescott arrived in Concord with the news that the British regulars were coming. By three or four, a messenger showed up at Robinson's house in Westford and informed him that the fateful day had arrived and the regulars were marching on Concord to search for arms. According to the recollections of Robinson's daughter, taken down when she herself was in her dotage, people began showing up at the house as he was making ready to leave. Robinson's only farewell to his wife was instructions to call up the girls and servants and have them cook provisions for the boys at the bridge. After he left, the women set about baking donuts, and they subsequently had a whole bushel sent down to Concord later that morning with a fourteen-year-old boy.

Before dawn, Robinson and his men gathered at the village green, at the muster field in front of the church. There was a brief moment of prayer for divine guidance, the so-called "artillery prayer," delivered by a patriotic clergyman named Joseph Thatcher, who was so taken with his invocation that he too marched off to join the fray. This was to be a fine little squabble, and if they meant to have a war, as the minutemen gathered at Lexington Green would be saying in just a few hours, then let it begin here.

Robinson, the ranking officer, set out for Concord on horseback. The others, 131 men of three companies, prepared to march.

By this time it was perhaps five or six in the morning, maybe later. But no doubt those living around Westford common, that is to say the Clevelands, the family of Aquila Underwood, Josiah Heald's family, and a few others, would have collected to watch the minuteman march off. It must have been enough to chill the blood—the dark figures milling and then forming into ranks, then the rattle of the drumroll, and the throbbing beat, and the fifes shrilling, and the shuffle of feet in the half-light of dawn. There is no record of this departure, but one imagines that a few of the young children and the wives followed after for some distance—down the Boston Poad, past the house of John Cleveland, past Providence Meadow on the north, past the house of Eben Spalding, and down through the orchard hills, the same ones that we ourselves so recently descended—to the Four Corners of the Boston and Littleton roads, where the house of Joseph Hildreth was located.

This mustering was a scene that, to varying degrees, was being repeated throughout Middlesex County and beyond. The alarm had spread. From Acton, from Sudbury, from Lincoln and Littleton, and Groton and Carlisle and Bedford, from every Middlesex village and farm, as Longfellow would tell it one hundred years later, one by one the little companies and contingents formed up, the so-called minutemen, each with his musket and shot, ready at a minute's notice. They had been practicing for this moment for over ten years, and now it was upon them.

For our part we push on, down Lyberty Way and across the grass between the parking lots of the new industrial buildings and on into the wild forest on the southwest side of the complex. Here, in the milkweed and asters and goldenrod that the mower failed to catch, monarch butterflies are feeding.

Monarchs, along with birds, are another one of those migratory animals that would seem to prove the theory of the biological origins of devotion to place. They weigh less than an ounce each, are subject to wind, rain, cold, predators, and starvation, and yet, each summer, instead of simply giving up and dying or, like their cousins, the mourning cloaks, hibernating, they set out for Michoacán in northern Mexico. Through hurricane season, through the storms and unsettled weather of the autumnal equinox, across the whole of New England, holing up periodically at their traditional migratory stopping places, at Delaware Bay, and again at the coasts of the Gulf of Mexico itself, they fly onward, until finally, their wings ragged, their lives half spent, they reach their destination—a singular mountain slope no more than fifty acres in total. Here, they will spend the winter, and then with the warming trends of late winter and spring, they will leave for the north. The individuals who make the southward journey do not live long enough to make it back to the sunny meadows where they were born. But the genes of their progeny remember and carry on the pilgrimage in place of their parents. Other than the eels, which undertake an odyssey in which they migrate some twelve hundred miles from Europe and America to the Sargasso Sea to breed, no creature of so supposedly limited an intelligence undertakes so vast a journey to so small a place. Only a fanatical devotion to a genetically ingrained domain could generate such a marathon trip.

The evidence of this deeply rooted natural conflict between devotion to a singular place and single-minded, determined journeying is all around us today. We enter the woods and move through an area of dense shrubbery of American filbert and winterberry, black alder, and spicebush, where now ragged violet leaves cling to grassy hummocks and wild grapevines hang from branches above us. We find boletes and puffballs, and a handsome purple mushroom that none of us can identify. Once again Barkley has been halted by bird life. Hermit and gray-cheeked thrushes pass by. He spots a vesper sparrow, a swallow calls overhead, tree sparrows are moving through, as well as white-crowned sparrows and phoebes. All of them are on the move to winter quarters, having deserted the places of their birth. They will be back next spring, though. They have all of North America, more or less, to choose from, and yet they will return to a spot no larger than one or two acres. And once settled in that place, they will defend their property to the edge of death. In the nineteenth century, ornithologists believed birds defended their territories out of love. Now we have come to believe that they fight for place, for *Lebensraum.*

BARBARA WILSON

JOSHUA TREE

OCK FACE
I am plastered to hardness, my face to burning hot boulder
face, my booted toes jammed in cracks, my fingertips poking
blindly in search of a hold. Splayed on the rock wall, I'm not as terrified
as I imagined I'd be; I'm more frustrated. I scrambled partway up out of
bravado, and now I'm stuck like a bug about to be smashed. My clothes
reek sourly in the heat, as if I hadn't washed for months, not just a few
days. Clinging to the side of the cliff, my armpits close to my nose, I smell
anxiety as well as sweat. I can't figure out a way to go up another step.

From below, Dana, our instructor, calls up, "Try that little crack to the
right. Can you get your toe wedged in over there?"

I see the crack; it's big enough to stuff with a thin notebook, not a boot
toe. My upper arms don't have enough strength to haul my weight over in
that direction. They feel like Jell-O. I mutter something despairing. I'm
hot. My knees are battered, and the toenails of my big toes are turning
black—I can feel them. I am angry and hot and sweating. I don't like
heights. But I am not afraid of that, strangely enough. After all, I'm staring

at a rock face, not measuring the length of a fall. And even if I did fall, I'd be okay; I am harnessed and belayed. I can feel the harness cutting into my crotch. No, I'm not afraid of falling. I'm afraid of my weakness. Of letting myself down. Letting Outward Bound down. Being the one who will not be able to do this terrible thing, make this climb.

Dana keeps on calling up calm advice. This crack. Or that one. Don't think too much. Trust and go. She has all the time in the world. But red-haired, emotional Sarah, anchoring me with blistering hands, suddenly shouts, "Trust your body, Barbara. Trust it."

Does anyone who's been abused trust her body? Or anyone else's? Or anyone? Much less anyone to hold her in belay, to hold her on the side of a cliff?

The Outward Bound catalog called it simply a Women's Course in Desert Backpacking at Joshua Tree National Park, in the Mojave Desert outside Palm Springs, California. A week in the high desert at wild-flower time, a week learning outdoor skills, living simply, sleeping under the stars. Rappelling was mentioned, I recall, and rock climbing. I passed mentally over those words in favor of "stark yet beautiful land-scape." I knew it would be hard, but then, I wanted it to be hard: a pilgrimage in search of something I didn't understand.

A pilgrimage with other women who also wanted and didn't want it to be hard.

The five of us flew in from far away; those from the East Coast left icy temperatures. They imagined balmy desert nights, sunny days to work on tans. We plaster ourselves with sunscreen during the day and wear sunglasses and hats. It is the high desert at the end of winter, bright with thin, cold air. We wear our thermal underwear almost all the time, and at night we put on layers and more layers, all we have, and get into our sleeping bags during dinner. In the morning there is ice on our sleeping bags. And a brightness that is almost too much to bear.

Nilda came from the Philippines as a young woman to marry a man she met in an ad. She is small and tough, upset with the others for using such vulgar language (*Fuck!* Andi screams while rock climbing. *Fuck fuck fuck!* So it rings out over the desert). She does yoga and is flexible; she looks like a snail with her huge black pack weighing her down. She chose an all-women's trip because "Men always think they know everything. Men always try to tell you what to do." She never speaks of her husband, who seems to be wealthy and retired, with any affection.

Sarah is married too, to a dentist in New York. She has two boys. She is close to my age but in much better shape. She says she exercises for hours every day to blow off steam, to get rid of her excess energy. She came on this all-women's trip because she was afraid that if there were men, she would fall in love. She tells us with a laugh, "I know myself. I'd be obsessed with being beautiful and attracting some young stud. My father died when I was ten and I've been falling in love ever since. I know myself. I don't need that." Sarah is the only one of us to try to keep up some semblance of attractiveness, which gets harder with each passing day. She puts on mascara every morning. She folds her bandanna in new ways; she wears her hat at a jaunty angle.

Andi wants to be the clown. Later she admits it's only nervousness that makes her crack constant jokes. She is the youngest and the slowest. "Pokey," her family called her. When everyone else has her pack on, Andi is still desperately looking for her toothbrush. She is strong and eager, the youngest, the chattiest. She signed up because she realized she had no friends who wanted to do the physical things that interested her.

Chandra wants transformation. She ended a long-term relationship not because she fell in love with someone else, but because she was yearning for something more. She has trained mightily for this trek to the desert, but physical challenge is not of great interest to her. When she climbs the cliff, she goes straight up, but she doesn't care to do it again. She came not to prove anything about her strength or agility but to discover more of who she is and might be. She has no patience when Andi and Sarah start talking about fashion and beauty. She wants to hit them. She has often wanted to fit in and "be nice" in her life, but she can sometimes be rude to the others. She is the first to go to bed after dinner. I know from the beginning that she will be my friend on the trip, though we don't talk much until the third or fourth day.

I don't understand entirely why I'm here. I have signed up for an Outward Bound women's trip when I could have spent the same money to live in luxury in Palm Springs for a week. I am the oldest and the least fit. I have trained for this trek by losing weight, walking five miles a day with a pack. By the time I left home, my pack weighed twenty pounds. I knew I wasn't prepared, but then, nothing could have prepared me. Everything that I fear and everything that is strong in me is here for me to look at and deal with.

By the time we come to the "boulder wonderland," where we will rock climb and rappel, we have been walking for three days. We've learned to read topographical maps and to find our way with compasses over ridges, saddles, peaks, and washes. Sarah navigates with me one day down from Quail Mountain, and Chandra another as we find our way through washes. We never walk on trails. We fan out across the desert in order to do as little damage as possible to the fragile ecology; we climb straight up mountains with sixty-pound packs full of cooking supplies, emergency gear, and climbing ropes. The water we carry is precious—and heavy. Under the weight of these huge black backpacks, we squeeze over and under giant boulders in washes buried by stone falls; we walk the sides of mountains, hugging invisible contour lines, trying to keep steady and not waste energy by going up or down in elevation.

The desert begins to seem familiar. Barrel cacti with their bright red blossoms, prickly pear, beavertail cactus. Mesquite, yucca, and a spiny plant called blackbrush, which from a distance looks like a spray of iron filings clustered on a magnet. In rock crevices are tiny, fat, succulent rosettes; and strewn carelessly everywhere are single wildflowers, blue and white mostly, and here and there a yellow or a bright red one. There is also, of course, the Joshua tree, which studs the desert and gives this particular place its name. The Joshua tree is not a tree but a shrub. It grows the way it does, tall and branched, like a Dr. Suess drawing, multi-limbed with tufts for hands, because of a weevil. It would like to grow straight, but the weevil irritates its very being, threatens its plant sanity. The Joshua tree, struggling to outrun the weevil, moves outward, building new plant cells that eventually form a new limb. It responds to pain and irritation by growing.

I am taking forever to get up this rock face. I am not good at climbing. My ankles are weak, my knees already creak from age, my arms have no strength. I am a big baby. I am an old woman. I should not have to do this. "Think about it, but not too much," Dana calls up, encouragingly, "and then move."

I call back down in frustration, after I have slipped from my hold three times in succession, "I know how to get there, but I can't get there."

"You're not putting everything into it."

I know and don't know what that means. After all, I am halfway up and somehow I got here. I hoisted and pushed and saw the right way for me and went. Tenderhearted Sarah wept for me when I got over the last rough spot, but now I am stuck again.

The method of Outward Bound is simple—to toss you in to the middle of something that seems impossible and then stay with you while you do it. Phoebe and Dana made climbing look so easy. Unharnessed, they scrambled up this rock face to set the course for us. They've already instructed us in knot tying, navigation by compass and map, stove lighting, and desert toiletry etiquette. We depend on them utterly, even though they keep telling us that by the end of the trip we will be depending on ourselves and one another. We adore them when we aren't hating them, when we don't imagine they are tormenting us for the sheer pleasure of seeing grown women weep.

They are younger than most of us—in my case, far younger. They live the kinds of lives that were made possible by their single mothers, by my generation of feminists. They live in their cars for periods when not working, bike around India, hike in New Zealand, rock climb for sport. They know how to take care of themselves in the wilderness, and although they are instructors on many types of Outward Bound courses, they like women's courses best because of the group spirit that develops, the support of women for one another, the personal transformation that often happens.

In the evening Phoebe sits around with some of us and tells long, slow, hilarious stories of her childhood in a hippie commune, and of her travels ever since. Dana goes off to be alone before sleep, to read and to write. Across our desert camp I see her bulked in her sleeping bag against the cold, her lamp illuminating the pale disk of her face.

I would like to be young again, young like *them,* strong and curious and unafraid. With all the world before me.

I have two stories I tell myself abut my body. One is that I always was an active child who loved to bike, roller skate, and swim. This child grew into a girl who excelled in modern dance classes and who wasn't bad at soccer and basketball. She became a young woman who rode her bike every day, who liked to dance, who could walk for miles. In her thirties she hiked in the Pyrenees and the Canadian Rockies, kayaked for a week off Vancouver Island.

The other story is of a child abused at age seven, who grew up without a clear sense of where she ended and where the rights of another person's desire began. A girl who early ran to fat and whose attempts at dieting kept pushing her weight up over the years. A girl who liked to lie around reading for hours at a time. A woman who had weak ankles and slightly creaky knees, who developed sciatica and asthma in her thirties.

Who pushed herself only up to a point and then began complaining.

Who was afraid of hurting her body. Who was afraid of pushing her body. Who was afraid of trusting her body.

Who was afraid.

Dana and Sarah are quiet down below. They are watching Andi, who is shouting out her own fear and frustration on a pitch some yards away from me.

"I want to give up," I call down peevishly. "I can't go any farther."

"Just try a little longer," says Dana, calm and kind. "I know you can do it."

I try and fail, making a small leap that has no juice in it. The harness cuts into my legs and crotch. I have only tried to show them I am a failure.

God, what a wimp I am. I am violently angry all of a sudden. *Oh, just fucking do it,* I think, *and shut up,* and I lash out at myself, at the rock, hot as metal and unyielding as memory. "Fucking hell," I mutter, and it echoes back at me.

I am up. Almost uncomprehending. Exuberant. How?

Dana cries, "Go, *girl!*" And Sarah doesn't cry for me this time—she cheers.

SOLO

The desert has a hallucinatory quality anyway, but there is something about living at the edge of one's ability that gives everything an added shimmer. The day after my rock climb I wake up feeling ill, but in no recognizable way. I don't have a cold or the flu. My bowels feel oddly shaky, dry. I am dizzy under the intense blue of the sky. I am probably dehydrated, says Dana, and she makes me drink a quart of water.

We are walking through a wash that runs among boulders of piled immensity: peach granite worn to shapes of bones and faces, thighs and animals. The wash is like a path of white sand in a painting by Piero della Francesca. Everything is clean and bright. The birds sing and the sky is a heartbreaking blue, with a pale circle of moon sitting on one of the boulder piles like a halo. No one has much energy today. We fall into pairs, wander and chat. We are walking on a floral carpet, punctuated with bobcat prints. Because of el Niño there has been an unusual amount of rain this year, and the water has pooled up in certain areas. Amazingly, a pair of mallards en route somewhere else have settled with delight into a pond in the shadow of the rocks.

Chandra tells me some of her life story, about her long relationship and the newness and strangeness of living alone. We exchange theories of why we're here, under this Giotto blue sky, walking endlessly through the desert. Why would we choose to spend money to be so uncomfortable, so fearful, so tired, and so cold? (Though at the moment we feel cheerful, and warm and relaxed.)

I say, "I wonder if we sometimes do a hard thing not in order to be able to do that hard thing again, but so that other hard things, or less hard things—the things we really want to do—will seem easy in comparison."

I know that I never want to rock climb again, and yet I am still lingering in the amazement of having done it at all.

"I had a moment," I explain, "When I wasn't myself, with all my fear and holding back—when I was just going up. When I was up."

The others are at a crossroads, peering at the map and deciding which direction to take. Chandra and I linger, with the sense of playing hooky, just for a minute. I take a closer look at a prickly pear, seemingly constructed of flat green pancakes, and at a beavertail cactus. In this clear hallucinatory air, it invites caressing, with its pale green skin and red soft spines. The cactus leaves are shaped less like beavertails than hearts. In each case, a fresh young "heart" is growing out of an old one, which dries and then crumbles around it.

The group ahead looks at us meaningfully: we're to speed up and join them. But Chandra says, "The hardest thing for me is to learn to be alone. I'm just realizing that I've never been without a partner in my life. I think I came to the desert to find that out. I want to be more alone than I am here. I don't want to be with all the others. I am so much looking forward to the solo. For the experience of being alone, completely alone, in the desert."

I too have begun to look forward to my solo time. A week ago I couldn't have imagined that twenty-four hours by myself in the desert with only water and a small bag of gorp would seem alluring. But I've had no time to myself for five days. Every minute has been accounted for; there's been little time to sit and dream. We are walking. We are climbing. We are unpacking and packing up, we are cooking, cleaning, practicing our knots. We are telling stories and working out how to live so closely with one another. We are sleeping.

Sitting in a circle now, listening to Dana and Phoebe explain how the solo works, how we will be out of sight of one another but not out of earshot, we look carefully at one another's faces, in respect and silence. We are asked what our fears are about being alone in the desert for a day and a night. I don't mention my worst one, the one I thought about at home in Seattle. The fear that a huge red-faced man with a greasy ponytail would roar up in his Harley Davidson or creep with a knife in his teeth through the mesquite in the dead of night, to rape and murder me.

Long ago, when I was small, my uncle went on a trip to Arizona with us and exposed himself to me in a secluded river canyon. That was the beginning of abuse that went on intermittently that summer. I don't remember much about it, and I began to remember it at all only as an adult. But I know that, always, my joy in being in the wilderness—or even on a lonely path in a city park—has been undercut by fear. Around any bend, along any stream, behind any tree there could be a man who intends to harm me. I have never slept outside, in the wilderness, by myself before. It was not something I could have imagined doing.

Dana leads Chandra and me silently to our "territories," where we will be for the next twenty-four hours. We are not to leave these spaces, which are bounded by a mesquite here, a wash there. The idea is not to go exploring but to sit and meditate. There's a whistle system to link us in case anyone gets in trouble. I find I have no fear as I nod good-bye to her and begin to set up my tent and organize my living space. The landscape of juniper, blackbush, and Joshua trees, of sandy wash and tan boulder piles, seems utterly familiar to me now.

I set up my tarp and unroll my sleeping bag, drink a little water. What next? It is so delightful not to be walking, not to be carrying a heavy pack, not to be doing anything. I stretch out on the sleeping bag under the blue sky and feel myself relax. Perhaps I'll just sleep for twenty-four hours. Suddenly I smell myself, and then, quickly, I rip off all my clothes. I can't wash them, but I can air them out. I drape my long underwear and shorts, my socks and T-shirt, over a mesquite bush.

I have so very rarely been naked outdoors. Not nearly often enough. Why am I not afraid? Why do I feel so free? And so safe? The air is delicious against my bare skin. There is no sense of separation. There's no real sense of self either. My two stories of myself as a physical being, as either active or fearful, have given way to an empty but curious mind, a sensation of wind on skin.

I want to do a great deal on my solo. I want to draw pictures. And think about my life. Do some writing. Dana and Phoebe have suggested several projects. One is to make a "regrets list," to pretend we are eighty-five and looking back on our lives. What are we sorry we didn't do? When I was fourteen I made a list of all the things I hoped to accomplish in future years. I wanted to travel, to write poetry, to live in Europe, to read all the classics ever written. I have done many of the things I imagined. Now I make another list. I shouldn't be surprised that it is still full of travel. A great desire to live in Buenos Aires possesses me temporarily. And then leaves. Once again, the desert is all there is. I don't really need to do anything more except be here, and look at the sky and feel the wind on my bare skin. When I am eighty-five I will have no regrets.

I am so tired that, after a tiny dinner of gorp and water, I fall asleep just after sundown. The moon is hidden behind clouds. I think briefly, *What if a bobcat comes and eats me?* I fall asleep before I can answer the question.

I wake once during night. The stars are out. Red stars and blue stars, the Twins and the Charioteer and every stud on Orion's belt. The dippers in the north sky carelessly scoop starlight. The moon is out, a silver lamp illuminating my tiny camp. I am alone, as alone as I have ever been. In whistling distance are the others, sleeping or waking, fearful perhaps, joyful and prayerful. I say a prayer, too.

I wake before dawn and watch the sky lighten from the warmth of my sleeping bag. I could stay here for another day, for a week. Not eating. A contemplative nun. My mind seems to expand, widthwise, so that I'm capable of holding different thoughts, separate but all visible at once. It's like the table function in a word-processing program. At age twenty I once took acid and drew a picture of the universe and my place in it. The next day I looked at this sketch only to find that it consisted of just a few arrows and a wobbly circle on the page. But my solo insights are calm and few; they seem to focus on the Joshua tree that anchors my tarp, that seems to dance like a Keith Haring figure in the clear morning sun.

The Joshua tree grows new limbs in response to the weevil of irritation, pain, and fear. It keeps growing in new directions.

THE VALLEY

It is raining on the last morning. We get up at 5:30 and pack up in order to make the pickup at 11:00. I'm expecting a brisk walk and then a harder section as we traverse a stretch of wash that will be, as Dana puts it, "a little choky." Meaning boulder-strewn. I'm expecting to have some last good conversations as we make our way to the bus that will take us back to the desert office of Outward Bound and then to the airport. My flight to Seattle is at 4:30, only eight or nine hours from now.

At first the dark, wet sky just makes everything more beautiful. The rain paints the barrel cactus a more luscious red, the boulders a duskier, delicious orange. I feel awake and capable, interested in the world, reluctant to leave the desert. Sarah and I walk together over the damp earth, talking about painting, wishing we had our watercolors with us. The wash we have entered is narrowing, the boulders pushing forward as if to claim our attention. We pick our way more carefully. The light rain begins to thicken and we hear water running. The rain gear I've been given is too large, the pants especially; their crotch hits me halfway down my thighs, and the rolled-up cuffs keep filling up with rain. Inside all these wet, stiff clothes, I have less agility than usual and feel that I can hardly raise my legs to step from boulder to boulder while keeping my balance under the huge pack that has gotten lighter but no smaller. My face and hands are soaked and cold.

And then the small, sandy trail that is the wash vanishes and we are dwarfed by gigantic wet boulders, some the size of cars, others like two-story houses. The rain pours down and the wash begins to run like the streambed it is, so that we also have to avoid stepping into ankle-deep water.

We all stop talking and concentrate on following Dana and Phoebe as they find their way forward. I'm not afraid, just disgruntled and uncomfortable. Until, while taking a long step down off a boulder, my pack pushes me forward and I pull the muscle behind my knee. The pain is quick and searing, and like a door it opens into a room of abject misery and anger at the *unfairness* of all this. I sit down abruptly like a two-year-old who's hurt herself, and two-year-old sobs suddenly well up loudly from my chest. I've had to do so many hard things in the last week: marching up and down ridges for eight hours a day with heavy water bottles in my pack, huddling at night from the cold, and waking up to ice on my sleeping bag; rock climbing, rappelling backward off a hundred-foot cliff. Today was supposed to be easy. This was supposed to be *over.*

I'm too miserable to be embarrassed. "My leg hurts," I sob. "It's too much." The others huddle around me. I hear someone say, "Let's lighten her load," and they take out the water bottles in the side pockets and a few things from the top of the pack. Dana looks at my knee and takes my hand to raise me up. "Can you go on?" she asks.

"Of course," I say. Because what else can I do? No helicopter is going to fly in and rescue me. One step at a time, I tell myself.

We all go on. For what feels like hours. Hours of rain and misery. At times we have to take off our packs and pass them down over huge boulders; at times we must crawl on our hands and knees through rock tunnels. It's clear that Dana and Phoebe weren't expecting this to be as hard as it is. Or were they? Is this our last test? I want to blame them, blame somebody. *It's not fair.*

Because I can't put my full weight on my knee, I continue to hold Dana's hand sometimes, when I'm traversing a ridge. Sometimes I sit down and slide, or pull myself with my arms across a boulder. I put my trust in Dana and will myself to believe that she knows exactly where she's going. I watch her feet and put my own where she has placed hers. I am not a trusting person. I especially don't trust people with my body. I have needed to protect myself, to learn self-sufficiency. That is another of my stories: where fear and independence come together. But I make the decision to give myself over to Dana, to let her lead me, to let her hold my hand through the worst of it.

Where are we and how long will it take? In the distance there is a wet blur of desert where presumably the van is now waiting for us. We are late and getting later. The rain pours down, gushes in gullies, and the water level is rising. *I must follow and believe,* I tell myself. It's no use being fearful or unafraid. It's no use calling on my willpower or my self-esteem. I've given all that up. I'm down to the bone. I'm soaking wet and weepy and worn and clear as glass. I will only follow Dana. Follow her and trust her; that's all I have to do, that and notice the horrible beauty of where we find ourselves. The contours of the massive stones and how they have been shaped by wind and occasional floods. The sound of water. The sky breaking its beakers over our heads.

When we finally emerge from this cascade of boulders we are forty-five minutes late for the pickup and there's no time to waste getting on the bus. Hardly any time to notice the lavish spill of blue and orange and white and yellow wildflowers around us. When we turn to look back at where we have come from, something more profound than pride takes hold of us. Awe. For the passageway looks majestic and menacing. How could we have managed to make our tiny way through that rocky hugeness? And a line from the Psalms comes to me:

"Yea, though I walk through the Valley of the Shadow of Death, Thou art with me," I think. *Thou* is Dana. *Thou* are the women traveling with me. *Thou* is myself. *Thou* is the boulders and the rain and the pain and the push; *thou* is all of it.

We sometimes do a hard thing—who knows why? To understand ourselves. To surprise ourselves. To redeem the past. To create the future. Should I take most pride in my rock climb, or in the humility that allowed me to let Dana lead me out of the Valley of the Shadow of Death? Shall I think back most to the moonlit heavens or the Giotto blue of the afternoon sun behind apricot piles of boulders? Or the warmth of my connection with women I never knew before, whose humor and strength got me through?

Since I've returned, I've found myself, at times, beginning to pull back from something that seems a little too hard or complicated, and then shrugging off my hesitation and moving ahead. I feel stronger, more agile. I feel I could do it again. And again. Grow new limbs and keep growing.

There was a moment—there were many moments on that pilgrimage away from fear or right into its heart—when my old, constructed stories fell away and I was no longer a brave, stubborn, active child, nor a timid and fearful one.

I was only desert wind on bare skin.

I was the moon and stars, a new heart emerging from a hardened cactus, a wash that was a path, a white path through a valley choked with old boulders.

WHEN MEN
AND MOUNTAINS MEET

T he road winding back to town from the cliffside guesthouse was lined with families camped out for the night. I woke before the others and went out into the hallway to a window. Darkness continued to simplify the valley. From the upper floors it was hard to pick out shapes. High on the ridge a few small campfires glimmered. A scattering of mountain-born Yemenis had pitched their tents along this jagged cliff, trading the soft sand for a perspective.

As the predawn call to prayer ran up the hill, lantern lights came on inside the tents. Gradually gray figures stepped out onto the rocks and formed neat rows. This narrow wedge of a view from one hall window was representative of the whole valley. The whole population of Mina would be on its feet now, three million people lining up *fajr* in the dark.

Throughout the guesthouse doors were clicking open. John Muhammad limped out of a bedroom, followed by Abd al-Qadir and Mardini. Usama appeared. Fayez looked wide awake.

The delegation filed into the hall, lined up on a rug, and faced Makkah. Nasser cleared his throat and began the call. Nasser's speaking voice was rough. It bounced along the corridor this morning like pea gravel strained through a bullhorn. But when he began to sing, it was angelic. I had heard my share of muezzins by now, but never one with such a clear vibrato. The Muslim *adhan* is a highly developed art form; Nasser's vocal talents were first-rate. What is more, for anyone who knew him, there was the added pleasure of so much tenderness pouring from a man with the voice of a Maxon. I never got used to it.

After breakfast we went downstairs with our passbooks. I carried mine in a shoulder bag today, along with four or five books, a packet of medicines, and a camera wrapped in a scarf to keep out sand. On top lay the player on which were recorded the prayers of all my friends in Marrakesh. As we moved outside, an officer noted the numbers in our passbooks. He examined the contents of my bag and waved me on.

The sheikhs had devised a careful plan to minimize exposure to the sun. The plan fell through the moment we left the building. Our vans, which ought to have met us at the door, were trapped in the valley. The road ahead lay choked with pilgrims. The guides formed a huddle. The huddle broke up. Nasser waved an arm. We began to walk.

At 7:00 A.M. all of Mina was in motion. Winding downhill to the parking lots, I had my first clear view of the whole valley: a mile-wide dun-colored corridor forming one continuous plane between two ranges, from its western edge against the spine of Makkah due east to Arafat, five miles away. The sky was still faintly pink in that direction, and traces of morning ground fog smudged the view. Past Muzdalifah the visible end of the valley tapered off most of the way the land ran with tents and glints of chrome.

I had been through Super Bowl gridlock in San Francisco. I knew the rush-hour tunnels of New York. I had witnessed Woodstock and marched on Washington. I had never experienced a throng approaching this one. It was as if the twentieth century's thickest tie-up had embarked on an epic journey back into Roman times. A tricky desert sky hung over everything, compressing volumes, curving distance, befuddling the eye.

As we boarded vans, a block-long hulk of yellow helicopter appeared above the cliffs over the road. It hovered long enough to drop a stretcher on a cable, then pluck a prostrate pilgrim from the crowds. It reeled him up and vanished over the hillside. Mardini referred to the craft as a flying hospital. The Saudi army had seven of these contraptions, with landing pads all over the valley.

We inched our way down the drive to Abdul Aziz Street. The encampments in this quarter were mostly filled with Pakistani peasants. The numbers of mothers with infants startled me. The hadj in July with a baby on each hip seemed inconceivable. Nasser guessed that the children were here because of economics. Their parents could not afford to leave them with nursemaids. (Taking a child on the hadj does not fulfill its obligation. Grace always attaches to the journey, but the rites are void without mature intent, or *niya*.)

The pressing heat and constant need for water weighed down older people, too. The camps were peppered with them, men and women seventy and eighty, bent over walking sticks, toothless, squinting. They were here by choice, of course, to do their duty and to soak up the hadj's grace before they died. The women looked bird-boned. The men in white towels, creaking down embankments, appeared to have one foot in the other world.

At the bottom of the hill the crowds thinned out, and the cars and trucks and buses and vans took over. We boarded our vehicles. For several minutes I saw nothing but steel hoods and blazing trunk lids. Then the road ran up into a viaduct and gave us a bird's-eye view of Mina Valley.

Night had all but erased the surrounding mountains. Now they dominated everything. Their bouldered bases tumbled to the sand's edge, forming up the narrows of the valley. The contrast of gray-blue rock on sable was exact, as if cut with a scalpel. Terraces in the rock face higher up formed tier upon tier of shelflike lofty bleachers holding single ranks of canvas tents. The shelves zagged like roads in a pit mine. The tents were distant flecks. The treeless ranges appeared to have poked up yesterday, but they held legends. The Prophet's cave on Mount Hira lay to our west. To the north stood Mount Thebir, where Abraham had gone to sacrifice his son, and where Gabriel had stopped him.

"Do people still go up there?"

"A lot of people go up there," Mardini said. "To visit the site."

"What is there?"

"A big, flat rock. Split in two, very cleanly."

"Does that mean something?"

"They say it's where Abraham dropped the knife, when the angel stopped him."

It was no surprise to find the father of ethical monotheism at Mina. Muslims, like everyone in the Middle East, see his life as a metaphor for universal guidance. In their view, Abraham's story had two phases: an initial stage in Palestine and a second one in the Hejaz. In many ways the hadj commemorates this final chapter: pilgrims leave their home (as he left Ur), resign themselves to a pure life (*ihram*), circle the shrine he built with his son, and run between the *mas'a* hills, like Hagar. Today we were trooping past Mount Thebir, another stage in the Abrahamic drama.

The van rolled down off the escarpment, taking a crossroad to the middle of the plain. Here we joined one of the many numbered ribbons of new pavement linking Mina to Muzdalifah and Arafat. These long, sand-leveed roads ran high and dry across the desert, like taffy, stretched out in the sun. They paralleled each other through the sand, splitting the valley in quarter-mile channels, so that crawling along at a snail's pace, we could gauge our progress by vans across the way on our left and right. Sometimes we saw whole vehicles. More often we made out only roofs, viewed over sand humps topped with hanks of thorn brush. There was something submarine about the valley. Low dunes lapped the canyon floor, as if a sea had boiled off it in the night.

A pedestrian walkway shaded with green roofing ran down the center of the plain. Thousands of hadjis flowed along it, keeping pace with the traffic, stirring up dust clouds. It ran unbroken for about three miles, dumping out crowds at the eastern end of the spillway. Seen from the air, the walkway would be a prominent feature. From the van it was hard to distinguish across the sand. Had Mardini not pointed it out, I might have missed it. It was difficult to hold any view in focus, especially where dust became involved. Heat waves curled off the sand. The sky was scored with corrugated ripples.

Where the valley narrowed, we crossed a riverbed, the Wadi Muhassir. Over its dry banks we joined a track reserved for special cars. The traffic gained speed here, in keeping with a tradition that the Prophet had spurred his camel through this pass.

The road climbed slightly, hills fell off to either side, and we entered the mile-wide basin of Muzdalifah. Again the valley ground was packed with tents, the hills dotted white like Mina's. In the acid light objects melted to shades of solar brown. Lost between slopes, a worn gray runner of masonry and stone wound through the clinkers. This was an eighth-century aqueduct built by Princess Zubaidah, wife of the caliph of Baghdad. Easing the hadj for centuries to come, Zubaidah had paid to sink a hundred wells from Kufa in southern Iraq all the way to Mina. She and her husband, Harun ar-Rashid, had performed the hadj nine times along this route, once across a field of carpets rolled out every morning on the sand.

We had traveled about four miles in two hours; it was nine o'clock when a chevron of army motorcycles appeared out of nowhere. Whether they were meant as an escort, no one knew. The sirens made one feel singled out. The touch of protocol just slowed us down. We crept through a crossroads. Soon we were mired in a major tie-up. The van sank down in the sunlight. The soldiers revved their bikes and roared away.

As often happened during stalls, John Muhammad and Abd al-Qadir began chanting. The rest of us sat looking through the windshield while three Turks jumped from the truck ahead and climbed onto its roof to survey the traffic. They squinted and shrugged and shook their heads and climbed down again. While we sat and sweated, a yellow school bus inched up beside us in the right-hand lane. Whenever its driver hit the brakes, they screeched like donkeys. The bus, a large old clunker, teetered with fifty pilgrims from the Punjab. Water bags hung from its bumpers. The rooftop luggage rack was full of men clutching umbrellas. They, too, were chanting "I am here."

Files of pedestrians swept by on roadside paths. Some waved staves with make-shift banners. With the men in *ihram*, it was hard to tell families apart or confirm nationalities. The banners helped to keep the groups together. I saw Moors from Spanish North Africa, Libyan Berbers, blacks from the Sudan, Syrians, Palestinians, Kurds and Iraqis, Mongols, Circassians, Persians, Baluchis, Afghans, Malays, and Sinhalese. I became so immersed in this pageant I did not mind our lack of forward progress. Even hadj congestion had a planetary character. The chunk of road we looked out on was as racially dense as a UN parking lot on Flag Day.

In a while the driver stepped down from the bus beside us, climbed onto the bumper, and raised the hood. Then he got down and untied a water bag on the fender. I saw him unscrew the cap and squint into the liquid, but instead of topping off the radiator, he made a circle around the bus, pouring water over all the tires. The passengers up on the roof strained forward, as if to will their old crate back to life. The rubber steamed. The driver slammed the hood and climbed back in.

The bus inched away by stages, and a TV truck began to take its place. The cabin of this vehicle bristled with aerials. On the bed in back two men worked their gear beneath a shade tarp. The camera lens peered out from the canvas, turning on a dolly. While it panned, an enormous Nigerian woman strode from the crowd, waving a handbag hoisted on a stick. It was strange to see pilgrims vie for the camera's attention. However, the main events of the hadj were broadcast live, all day, around the world, and everyone knew it. These people were waving, by prearranged signals, to watchful families thousands of miles away. My friend Qadisha, I now remembered, had urged me to carry a bright purple umbrella, hoping that it would help me to stand out. I waved to her three or four times as the truck crawled forward.

We were heading toward a boundary line that divided Muzdalifah from the plains. Arafat proper, the site of the hadj, lay a mile away. As the van gained ground, the enclosing ranges tapered, then opened like an hourglass below the waist. We passed a pair of whitewashed pillars at the mouth of the valley, marking the edge of sacred territory. Another dry river, the Wadi 'l-Arak, extended for some distance to our left. It was filled with a shrub that the Makkans prize for toothpicks. Behind sparse green tops we picked out the spires of Namira mosque farther down the valley. Its minarets stood out like ships' masts in a harbor. There were four.

The enormity of my assumption, that words could take the measure of the hadj, caught up to me on the Plain of Arafat. I saw now why men as observant as Rutter and Burckhardt had given it two pages. At Arafat the hadj became too big to be a subject, too sprawling, too amoebic. There were no hooks by which to hoist the vista. Its edges outran the verbal frames we place around things. Its center was everywhere, confounding reason, opening the heart.

The four-mile bowl of sand we entered now was lined with tents enclosed by granite mountains, identical white canvas rows, forming quads that lapped out of sight, fusing into dots on the horizon. Sweeps of momentarily homeless millions were divided here and there by two-lane roads winding through the camp like canals through Venice, coming and going in the mist. As we rolled to a stop in one of these canvas rivers, I gave up and slipped my notebook into my bag. I relinquished my post at the fort of objective inquiry. Chants of "labbayk" welled up from the plain.

The van rocked and pitched as we watched at the windows.

> *You wanted a look*
> *At Death*
> >   *before you faced it?*
> *Now you have seen it*
> *with your eyes.* (Qur'an 3:143)

If Arafat was a dress rehearsal for Judgment Day, one thing seemed certain: no one would be alone there. The crowds on the road gleamed like figures from two worlds. The hadj was at its most ethereal right now, vibrating between the real and the symbolic. Out on the sand a man in towels marched past the van with a green flag. Suddenly it was as if we had driven into a Wallace Stevens poem. The figures in the street became figures of heaven. Men grew small in the distances of space. The blown banners seemed to change to wings. Then the van jerked suddenly forward, the crowd swam into focus, and we floated along together down the plain.

The plain is not entirely a desert. At the eastern end of Orina Valley, I caught a glimpse of some leafy, planted rows bounding the long west wall of Namira mosque. This stretch of verdant farmland shocked the eye after what we'd come through. In the sixteenth century all of Arafat was cultivated. Today we had this tidy patch of green, dwarfed by lunar sweeps of barren gravel. The garden only added to the land's surreal aspect, bean rows jutting up from nowhere, flanked by boulders shaped like body parts. The only missing touch was the Daliesque pocket watch.

A few blocks from the mosque our driver nosed the van into the wrong end of a blacktopped one-way alley lined with buses. This aisle was fitted out to form a market. Tents on either side were jammed by pilgrims buying juice and fruit and small provisions—bread, umbrellas, head cloths, beads, canteens. People beyond the berms of the road looked blissful, complacent. On the pavement, however, a heated throng of shoppers bulged onto the road and blocked the way. Ahead a man on a crooked staff had fallen to his knees, and a crush of sheep and hadjis stood around him. Muhammad once called pilgrimage an "honorable equivalent of battle." From here it had all the tumult of a campaign.

I wanted badly to get out and walk now. We hadn't moved a yard in fifteen minutes. The Namira mosque was the same distance away. When Nasser barked an order and the long side door rolled back, I got to my feet. A gust of fresh air blew through the cabin. Before I could move, however, the van lurched forward and the door slammed shut. Our driver had found a gap in the oncoming traffic and was gunning the engine, bouncing down a sidetrack, honking, shouting. The delegation cheered. Rounding the mosque, he swung a hard right and rejoined the traffic. We continued nudging forward through the crowd.

The roads were little veins of pandemonium in the larger, calmer body of the hadj. Once we had found our parking lot and left the van behind, I marveled at the quiet in the campsites. Laid out in quads, they occupied the largest part of the valley; the roads were no more than perimeter stripes around them. Each quad was further broken into blocks, great sandy courtyards edged by canvas tents and gravel walkways. The tents sat backed against these paths. Stalls and vendors collected at each crossroads.

In contrast to the roads, the camps felt cool and crisp and organized. Here life's minor rhythms carried on. A young man crouched to wash at a plastic bucket. Three Iraqi women sat around a Primus stove, sipping coffee. A baby whimpered.

The first real breeze in a week blew down the valley. It whipped up scraps of paper as we walked. The air smelted strongly of ozone. Tissue-thin, high clouds dulled the sun. After ten days and nights in the hollow, the plain felt cool. It was ninety-three degrees Fahrenheit at ten-thirty, a low unheard of in summertime Makkah. Usama, in particular, looked relieved. Yesterday at the guesthouse he had been dying. Now he kept pace with the sheikhs as they marched along. A few rows back came Abd al-Qadir and Ahmad, forming their usual guard for John Mohammad. John walked with a shuffle. Ahmad held an umbrella above his head.

It was impossible to place ourselves in relation to the landscape. The corridors of tents blocked any view. Cut off, with no point of reference, I wondered if it were possible to attend the hadj and miss it. Passing a rank of buses by the road, I stopped to look. They were locked, painted white, with sky-blue trim. At the back of one a ladder ran up to the baggage racks. I let the others pass and climbed the ladder. From the roof, I had a good view of Jabal al-Rahmah.

It lay at the closed end of the valley, butted against the foot of Mount

Namira. Broad stone steps zagged up the eastern side to a gentle summit two hundred feet above the plain. This modest pile of boulders was the focal point of the hadj. Every structure on the plain, tents included, faced or flowed toward it. A tall, whitewashed obelisk marked the summit. It looked the size of a matchstick from the bus.

I felt oriented the moment I saw Jabal al-Rahmah. The name means "Mount of Mercy. " Hadj encampments ran right up to its sides.

I had a long look, then caught up to the others, following Ahmad's umbrella to a pavilion. Nasser was making a speech when I came in. Men milled about him idly, listening, blinking, adjusting to the light. The enclosure was simple: a sixty-by-ninety-foot roof on concrete pillars, open on three sides but casting shade. A low wall ran around it. Nine-by-twelve red carpets lay on gravel. The gravel was level, loosely packed, and gave with a little crunch when I sat down. To the rear, behind tall screens, there lay a kitchen. Stacks of dishware rattled. Fans churned above me. The shade made the air delicious.

Nasser concluded his speech by announcing that this would be our base camp until nightfall. He warned us twice to stay out of the sun.

The pavilion was out of earshot of the traffic. With an hour until *zuhr*, the delegation lounged. A few told beads. Others read or talked. I was lying on a carpet reading supplications from a handbook ("We have halted in your courtyard," one began), when Abd al-Qadir and Dr. 'Ali, a delegate from West Africa, started talking. They were seated on either side of me. Their conversation, taking place across my body, resembled a Platonic dialogue.

Abd al-Qadir was pondering human suffering. He had seen, on the TV news the night before, some film clips of forest fires in California. The hills around Santa Barbara had been burning for a week, and hundreds of homes had gone up in flames, leaving families homeless. Tragic news on a holiday like this one—it nagged Abd al-Qadir. He asked 'Ali whether God created evil.

'Ali replied that God created everything. "The good, the bad, the whole shebang," he smiled.

Dr. 'Ali was an elderly Ghanaian lately relocated in Detroit. He spoke butter-smooth Gold Coast English and possessed a sweetness of disposition that intrigued me. He had a way of beguiling people while holding them at bay with his confident firmness. Though he rarely spoke much to anyone, I had seen total strangers cross crowded rooms to shake his hand, perhaps in the hope of absorbing his charisma. I never learned what his degree was in. 'Ali was a doctor of something very attractive.

Hearing that good and evil derived from Allah, Abd al-Qadir fell silent for a time.

"Maybe there's no such thing," he finally said.

"No such thing as what?"

"As evil."

"You are wrong," 'Ali replied. "God created the evils of air and water, for example."

"Of the air?"

"Tornadoes, for instance."

"A tornado isn't evil."

"Oh, yes," 'Ali said in his gentle way, raising a finger. "Crops are destroyed. People suffer. Children die. It is bad. And men feel badly."

"But tornadoes are made by pressure, not by evil. Name one thing that's really evil."

'Ali shook his head at this. "Bad things *do* happen. And people feel awful because of them. When one of the Prophet's children died, he wept. The others said, 'Why are you crying? It is God's will.' The Prophet said, 'God put mercy in our hearts. We are human beings.' If a city burns down, and no one mourns, it would be as if nothing had happened."

'Ali smiled sweetly while Abd al-Qadir chewed this over.

"But why would Allah make evil?" Abd al-Qadir asked.

"Perhaps as a way of telling people apart."

The sun angling over the roof put the grounds in shadow. The pavilion rippled beneath the fans. A little while before the call to prayer, I walked across the road in search of a bathroom. I needed to wash up before *salat*, and I wanted cold liquid. Even in the shade a liter of iced water turned tepid quickly. The bottles provided on our arrival were now hot to the touch.

Nasser asked where I was going, and I told him. He gave me an umbrella (Hadj law forbids male pilgrims to cover their heads, but umbrellas have always been permitted. Being much larger in the old days, perhaps they were classified as tents. Burckhardt mentions a group of several thousand men under green umbrellas. At a distance, mounted on camels, they "bore some resemblance to a verdant plain.").

It is a whimsical pastime, strolling around in bone-dry heat beneath a cloudless sky with your parasol open. The breeze had picked up. The ruler-straight gravel lanes were mostly deserted. They intersected every twenty yards, forming mazy corridors of canvas. A cinder block latrine rose on my right. Inside, the walls were dotted with brass spigots. Men crouched in the shadows, washing. Others waited. A cement trough carried off excess water. The room was dark.

Outside again I paused on the stoop to let my eyes adjust. The plain appeared as a sheet of white-hot metal. It put me in mind of Valéry's motto for a sundial: "Lux dux." I was still getting used to it when a tiny man stepped up and squeezed under my umbrella. Withered and toothless, he took up so little room I hardly noticed. He carried a basket of oranges on his arm and while we stood there began nonchalantly handing fruit to the men emerging from the building. It was the sort of small, inspired gesture that so often endeared me to Islam. No one could have mistaken him for a vendor. He smacked his lips. He glanced away when someone thanked him.

Walking back, I passed a drink cooler on a picnic table. It was filled to the top with bottles, cans, and ice. This gleaming, snow-capped mound looked out of place here on the desert. The table was untended, the ice audibly meeting around the drinks. I worked a liter of orangeade free. I laid my hand on the ice until it ached.

By the time I reached the shelter, the call to prayer had started. The delegation stood facing Makkah. As prayers began, a low, steady hum engulfed the plain. A few million people were whispering in concert. A soft roar beat about the edges of the shelter.

The brevity of the session was exceptional. At Arafat *zuhr* and *'asr* prayers are joined and shortened. Instead of eight *rak'ahs*, today we made four—two groups of two cycles, with a third call from the minaret between. Prayer requires *wudu'* and *wudu'* requires water, which in the old days camels lugged over the plain. Condensing the sessions cut these needs by half. It also gave people an unbroken afternoon to use as they pleased on this day of days, and extra time before dusk to prepare an exit.

"You saw the roads this morning?" Mardini asked.

"Yes."

"Well, that was nothing."

"You mean everyone leaves at once?"

He said, "They try."

I remembered the recording of the prayers from Marrakesh. Preparing to play it, I fished the recorder from my bag and switched it on when the air around the pavilion roared with static. A moment later the voice of the imam of Makkah shook the plain. I knew this must be the Arafat sermon, but I had not expected it so early. I fumbled a blank cassette into the recorder and passed Mardini the tiny microphone.

Later, replaying his translation, the imam's voice overrode everything. It ran out at the top of his lungs for forty minutes, full of advice and theatrical emotion, sometimes breaking into tears. The delegation listened solemnly. The hectoring tone disturbed me. Loudspeakers boomed above the quads.

The imam's address was an annual occasion. It marked a brief, more memorable sermon made by Muhammad on the Farewell Hadj. This was the Prophet's last public speech. Deservedly famous, its contents are memorized by schoolboys. I had seen the words on plaques in Moroccan homes. The first lines made it clear that he knew he was dying:

Listen closely, people. I do not know if I will meet you here next year. From this day forward, until you meet your Lord . . .

In taking his leave, he abolished blood feuds and usury between Muslims. He exhorted people to stay together after his death. He reminded couples to honor their spouses and to use reason:

Listen to what I am telling you. Any Muslim is a brother to every other. Only take from one another things that are freely given. And do not do injustice to yourselves.

Muhammad had stood near the peak of Jabal al-Rahmah. The crier Rabi'ah stood below him, repeating his words to criers on the plain. The amplifiers replacing this ancient system were no great improvement. As often happened in the Middle East, the volume was turned too high. The speech sounded shattered.

After the sermon our rows broke into smaller groups. Dishware clattered behind the kitchen screens, then a group of Saudi boys in *thobes* appeared. They carried yard-long cylinders of white cloth in their arms, dumping them down like firewood at one end of the shelter, rolling them out on the carpet with soft kicks. Platters of food were placed on these improvised tables. We scooted into lines and began to esat. The meal consisted of curried rice and lamb shanks, bowls full of oranges and bananas, water, green coffee, cups of tea. The desert receded. For an hour the hadj became a communal picnic. "Once you eat in a place, you belong there," 'Ali said. Sheikh Nasser nodded.

The combined effect of the food and heat was stunning. A handful of pilgrims nodded off. Fayez and Fazeel, at opposite ends of the shelter, recited to themselves from bin Baz's book. There was little movement on the rugs between. As the day settled over us, I took out my camera and snapped several photos. A few men in our party objected to portraits, on the grounds that Islam's taboo against icons extended even to likenesses by Kodak. Most people had cameras of their own.

In a little while Mardini came over to borrow my radio. He was going for a stroll, to visit a tentful of notables, and he wanted to monitor the hadj as he walked along. I was feeling the heat by then and declined to go with him.

The blue sky past the roof looked painted, static. The black fan blades in the ceiling barely turned. I felt no desire now to move at all. If the pilgrimage had a pinnacle, we were on it. The sun appeared pinned into place, the mica glinted. In the prairie quiet the protean hadj became a vigil.

People may do as they like at Arafat. There is no required liturgy, no clutter. The point of the day is to be here. To inhabit the plain is sufficient. You may talk if you wish, or walk, or pray, or chant, or doze. There is nothing compulsory, no set pattern of behavior. No special spot to flock to. No metaphors, no verbs.

The *wukuf* is a chance to let the spirit breathe. For men like Fayez, it was also a day of answered prayers and God's rewards. They bent to their job, not wasting a moment, seeking blessings for friends and families. Hassan Mubarak, who worked in Detroit at the Clare Muhammed School, borrowed my Qur'an and lay down to read. Fazeel sat chanting. Dr. 'Ali fingered beads. I did an amount of all these things, then played back the Marrakeshis' prayer tape. Their familiar voices blended with the murmurs on the plain.

When the pebbled carpets became too hard to sit, I moved around the shelter, working out creaks, performing knee bends. At one point I crouched beside Fazeel. He glanced up from his chanting, cotton mouthed, and squinted at me in a distant way. I passed what remained of the orangeade. He drank it off.

"Is there more?"

I pointed across the road.

Soon we were weaving through the solar flares. Fazeel, I noticed, was as high as a kite from the chanting. He walked with a rolling motion, looking glassy. All at once a brisk wind came down the plain and tore the umbrella from his fingers. I chased it briefly, then we watched it go, tumbling inside out across the sand.

We returned with a half dozen soft drinks and distributed them to the men. By now I had run through my store of supplications. While the others prayed or chatted, I puttered for fifteen minutes, straightening rug ends, depositing empty bottles in a trash bin. I checked on John Muhammad. I gave him a tablet. I noticed a pilgrim getting up to leave.

Abd al-Mu'id was an interesting case—an Algerian computer engineer who lived in Colorado. That summer, after four confusing years, his marriage to an American was ending. The rift had begun when his wife joined a Bible group. It ended one night in his living room with the group trying to convert him to being Baptist. Abd al-Mu'id had confided to me that his hadj was a declaration. He had come here to get back in touch with who he was. He alone among our group had revealed a deeper motive to his journey. I watched him leaving the pavilion. I was tired of sitting on gravel, cut off from the crowds. Telling myself that he might get lost, I followed Abd al-Mu'id.

He turned down a corridor, walking toward Jabal al-Rahmah. The backs of the tents faced us here, the stays hammered into the sand formed vacant alleys. Again I was struck by an absence of commotion. The air hummed with a muffled drone. The tents faced inward on their courtyards. Directly ahead I saw only Abd al-Mu'id. His gait was easy. His white umbrella bobbed.

Following behind at fifty yards, I passed a group of air-conditioned tents with half-ton units pumping from their backsides. These intrigued me, God knows why, and I stopped long enough to peek into a tent through a chink in the canvas. The enclosure was empty, the hot air musty. The air conditioner was running at full blast.

When I turned back up the path, Abd al-Mu'id was gone. Now I remembered Nasser's warning about the sun. Seeing a clump of movement in the distance, I walked toward it. I was weaving from side to side to get my bearings, like an ant on a blueprint. The corridors cut by the tents curved in the heat.

At a road intersecting two camps, a government truck had backed into the road, and three soldiers stood on the tailgate, handing bags of water down the sides. Around them fifty or sixty hadjis reached up for the water. It came in shapeless packets, small and clear and blue when the sunlight hit them, and stamped in three languages: DRINKING WATER. GIFT OF KING FAHD. A soldier on the truck tossed me down a liter. I nipped the plastic end and drank it off.

I stopped at every crossroads to look for Abd al-Mu'id. The lanes between the tents were becoming more populous. Soon I entered a Pakistani quad. *Chipati* (flat-bread) stalls marked out the border. I peeked into one of the courtyards, where men and women lounged on carpets, shaded by orange saris propped on poles. They looked self-absorbed or relaxed to the point of dozing. A few sipped tea from bowls.

The Pakistani enclave continued for three blocks, then gave way to a district of Moroccans. The bakery odors turned to savory drafts of stewed tajine. Cheekbones changed. Tea was served in glasses jammed with mint. This was like stumbling onto a wedge of the old Maghreb, and I crouched beside a flap to take it in. At Mina, where tents served as private dwellings, I might have been run off for trespassing. Here no one noticed. I made a rapid once-over of the crowd, then looked closer. I was searching for someone, I dimly realized. In an attack of misplaced nostalgia I was combing the yard for Abd al-Hadi, the electrician from Marrakesh. At this realization I backed away from the tents, shaking my head.

The camps continued on for fifteen minutes. Every few blocks another ethnic margin marked a clear-cut border as I walked, like bands in a rainbow. Little India led on to Little Egypt. I looked up again and found myself in Thailand. In each case the plain *ihram*, designed to wipe out class distinction, heightened the contrast, setting races naturally apart. This was the mosaic that Malcolm X remembered:

There was a color pattern in the huge crowds. Once I happened to notice this, I closely observed it thereafter. Being from America made me intensely sensitive to matters of color. I saw that people who looked alike drew together and most of the time stayed together. This was entirely voluntary—there being no other reason for it. But Africans were with North Africans. Pakistanis were with Pakistanis. And so on. I tucked it into my mind that when I returned home I would tell Americans this observation; that where true brotherhood existed among all colors, where no one felt segregated, where there was no "superiority" complex, no "inferiority" complex—then voluntarily, naturally, people of the same kind felt drawn together by that which they had in common.

I was now on one of a dozen lanes that ran like spokes toward Mount Mercy. Wider than the aisles through the camps, these lanes were filled with hadjis like myself from the back of the enclave. Although the whole plain was Arafat, the jabal represented the heart of the action. Muhammad had stood on its peak. People wanted to see it.

A ring road circled the hill's perimeter. It looked less like a road from where I stood than like a moat full of shepherds. Ahead the feeder lane was a lake of hands. Another government water truck had backed into the road, and hadjis stood around it with their arms raised. I worked my way past them, wading through cast-off plastic. On the other side I stood facing the mountain.

Broad stone steps ran up the southern flank, making a left, then a right-hand turn, leading to the summit with its column. Halfway up lay a pad with a wall around it. This, it was said, marked a spot where the prophet Adam first performed *salat* (The name Arafat derives from a root meaning "to find, recognize, or know." It denotes the spot where, after their expulsion from the garden, Adam and Eve crossed paths and became reacquainted—a primal lost-and-found for souls). Hadjis leaned at the wall, enjoying the view there.

Earlier that week I had visited this hill when no one was on it. Now small figures perched on every rock. Some stood still like sentries, faces growing smaller near the summit. Others chatted under parasols or read from prayer books. Every few minutes a patch of two hundred people would stand together, wave their shoulder towels, and chant, *"Labbayk! Allahummah, Labbayk!"* An answering chorus rose up off the plain.

Behind the hill a higher shelf of cliffs overlooked the quads. It formed a gallery fringed with tents and cars, where hundreds of thousands of locals were assembled. Makkans considered these perches the best seats in the house, and they drove out from town in packs to claim them early. Shafeeq and Saleem were probably up there now, camped under a lean-to near his Brougham. Their view across the plains would be superb.

Very few tents stood on the *jabal* proper. Bodies packed the rocks on every side, but the slopes were too oddly pitched for real camping, and the boulders looked jagged. A few stunted mimosas poked through cracks.

On the outer rim of the road the crowds grew thinner. There were unexpected pockets of open ground and no trucks or cars. People strolled easily. Some walked arm in arm. Here and there I heard a vendor calling. Just then the crowd was moving in a counterclockwise direction, but this resemblance to the ritual *tawaf* was coincidental. Circling Jabal al-Rahmah was not a required rite of the hadj. A minute later the crowd's flow changed direction. Something offhand, even idle, about the procession distinguished it from the purposeful *tawaf.*

On the inner edge of the road, near the base of the hill, emotions ran higher. Walking there, I passed a dozen Filipino women. They were weeping. Farther on a distracted Kazakh pilgrim in a brilliant hennaed beard stood lost in meditation by the road. On the hill itself blocks of *ihrams* went up, and the chanting swelled in sections. Mount Mercy induced a notable self-effacing ardor. The nearer I came, the more my mind went blank and the place took over.

I continued around the drive and soon crossed paths with an old Yemeni woman selling apples. Remembering events at the latrine, I impulsively bought all the woman's fruit and walked along the road passing them out. The apples were small and red, perhaps from San'a. They gave my hands something to do while I strolled around. For all its ecstatic potential, the mood at this acme of the hadj was self-possessed, not at all trancelike. Now and then I felt a swell move through us—the unifying agency of the hadj.

Time passed quickly at the mountain. When my supply of fruit ran out, I started winding back to the pavilion. The sky grew hazy as I went. The sun declined toward the Makkan hills.

IONA

Whan that Aprill with his shoures soote
The droghte of March hath perced to the roote,
Thanne longen folk to goon on pilgrimages.

—The Canterbury Tales

I t is an Indian tradition that when you are fifty you should go on a pilgrimage, so in the summer of 1985 I began thinking and planning for a pilgrimage to the holy places of Britain the following year. I put a small advertisement in the personal columns of *Resurgence* [the magazine I edit] to see if there were any *Resurgence* readers who would offer me a bed for the night. There was such a tremendous response that when I set out I had an offer of hospitality in most of the places I was to visit.

My plan was to start at nine o'clock in the morning and to arrive at my host's house between 4:00 P.M. and 6:00 P.M. With a few exceptions, I aimed at walking every day, covering twenty miles per day on average, but a shorter distance for the first few days.

I started out with a small rucksack, one change of clothes, and the pair of Polish shoes I had on. I took no book, no diary, no camera, and as on my earlier walk from India to America, no money. Pilgrimage is best when you are traveling light, especially if you are walking.

On March 31, Easter Monday, I set off with my family toward St. Nectan's Holy Well at Stoke, two miles from Hartland.

———

The tradition of going on a pilgrimage is common to all religions. The Muslims go to Mecca, the Christians go to Canterbury or Jerusalem, and Hindus go to the source of the Ganges in the Himalayas. My mother used to say that if you haven't been on a pilgrimage by the time you are fifty, then your time is up: you mustn't put it off any longer. By the time you are fifty you have performed your essential duties in this world. You have paid off your mortgage to the building society and seen your children through school. You have given enough attention to your family and your business; now is the time to pay attention to your soul, your spirit, your imagination, and your creativity. From now on whatever you do should be in the service of the spirit. So pilgrims' routes have become established throughout the world. It was a great delight to walk that ancient path to Canterbury in my fiftieth year.

According to Jain custom, the birthday is the day of conception: you are born into the womb of your mother, and you exist from then on. So I was making my pilgrimage between the anniversary of the day of my conception and that of the day of my birth. If I was in India, I would have gone to the holy places of many Indian religions. I would have gone to Ajmer to be inspired by the teachings of the prophet Mohammed, the prophet of peace—Islam means "in peace." I would have gone to Bodh Gaya, the place of the enlightenment of Lord Buddha, the Lord of Compassion. I would have gone to Rajgir, where the founder of the Jain religion, Mahavir, taught the sacred nature of all creation. I would have gone to Kerala, where St. Thomas brought the teachings of Jesus, the Lord of Love. I would have gone to Gokul, the home of Lord Krishna, the Lord of Joy and Celebration, and I would have gone to Ayodhya, where Rama, the Lord of Right Living, reigned. But I was not in India, I was in Britain, and therefore I went to the holy Christian places, to stone circles and ancient springs.

In India, before you enter a temple you go around it. There is a precinct for that purpose, and by going once, twice, three times around you prepare and center yourself. You leave your negative thoughts behind. When your body, mind, and heart are ready, then you may enter the temple. Similarly, I was making a journey around the temple of Britain, so that I might enter into its mysteries. This pilgrimage was a pilgrimage to Britain, to its rivers, hills, moors, dales, fields, to all its natural beauty. Walking every day would take me four months. In India people go on pilgrimage for a week, or a month, for a year, or even more; I know four women pilgrims who walked together the length and breadth of India, taking twelve years.

In Canterbury Cathedral there is an area designated for silent prayer and meditation where pilgrims light a candle. In this dark corner of the cathedral, lit only by the many candles, I too lit a candle and said the Prayer for Peace. After giving his blessings, Canon Brett led me to the chapel of Saint Thomas à Becket. Although modernized, the chapel has an atmosphere of martyrdom, the sword hanging above the altar speaking the language of power and pain. I stood in silence and astonishment as Canon Brett told me the story. King Henry II had wanted to break the power of the church and so had appointed his friend Becket as archbishop of Canterbury in 1162. But when Thomas took his place in Canterbury, his inner voice told him that he must be true to God, and being true to God brought him in conflict with the king. In exasperation, a drunken Henry said one day at dinner, "Will no one revenge me of the injuries I have sustained from one turbulent priest?" The archbishop knew that knights were coming to kill him. His monks urged him to hide or escape or to order them to resist. The archbishop was unperturbed. He said calmly, "Why should I hide? I am not afraid of death. One thing is certain, all of us will die one day; no need to hide or escape. As for resistance, we are not here to resist but to suffer. We will not take life, we will offer our life." And so Thomas à Becket died at the altar and became a martyr.

But when the king heard that his knights had actually killed Thomas, he wept. The sacrifice of Thomas à Becket transformed the king: Henry repented, and walking on his knees became the first pilgrim to Canterbury.

Listening to this story I felt my doubts and hesitation vanish, my preoccupation with home, work, and worldly responsibility diminish. The tale of Thomas à Becket's fearlessness and detachment created a moment of breakthrough for me.

This breakthrough was further consolidated when I crossed the Thames estuary by boat. Being in the water gave me the sensation of being away from the earth, sailing away, leaving the world behind.

There is no longer a ferry between Faversham and Southend-on-Sea. The usual route to Ely would have taken me to London and through the Dartford tunnel. I had all along tried to avoid walking through the busy streets of London. So, thanks to John Harrison, I was able to cross the wide Thames estuary on a personal ferry: *The Orcades,* the home of Andrew Kennedy and Stevie, who make their living as painters using watercolor and oil. *The Orcades* is generally anchored off Rochester, and it came to Faversham to take me across the estuary under sail. I was expecting a crossing of a couple of hours, but the weather was rough, the wind was blowing, the waves were high, and the rain was tapping on the roof. When we arrived at Southend Pier seven hours later, at 6:00 P.M., the sky was heavy with dark clouds. I was in the midst of a roaring thunderstorm, with dazzling lightning and heavy rain. Southend Pier had suffered from fire a few years before and was still black, charred, and deserted. There was only one rusty, broken, and slippery flight of steps left. With pounding heart and shivering body, I walked the one-and-a-quarter-mile-long pier.

By the time I arrived at the house of my hostess, Hazel Grimsdale, I could see a glimpse of the evening sun, which was about to set, and a patch of blue sky behind the clouds. The wind was dropping. Hazel said, "You couldn't have chosen a worse day to sail." But I disagreed, saying, "I would not have missed this experience at any price." When one is in a house, one wants to avoid the rain, the wind, the thunder and lightning.

But when I was in that storm, the experience of the elements was physically and spiritually exhilarating.

———

Almost six miles before reaching Ely I could see the faint outline of the great cathedral, and as I walked closer and closer, the grandeur of this magnificent holy place of pilgrimage slowly revealed itself. This day's walk felt easy. The riverbank was soft and level, but more than that I felt I was being pulled by the power of the cathedral. By the time I arrived in Ely, I was already so much immersed in the visual and emotional experience of the cathedral that I felt I knew it intimately.

Entrance to this holy place of pilgrims and visitors was no longer free, and when I urged the box office clerk to let me, as a penniless pilgrim, go and offer my prayers before the altar, I was told that no exception could be made. As I looked at those who were permitted inside holding their tickets, eating ice-cream cones, treating the building as a historic monument, a museum, reading up on its facts and figures, it seemed to me that spiritual experience was perhaps easier to find outside rather than inside its walls.

I followed the river Gapping Way to Ipswich, visiting the country churches en route to Brinkley near Newmarket, Ickworth Park near Bury St. Edmunds, and Bucks Hall near Stowmarket.

It was always an interesting exercise to seek and find little footpaths and narrow country lanes, sometimes tarmac and sometimes dirt tracks. The Landranger series of Ordnance Survey maps is excellent for this purpose. I could not carry all the relevant maps with me, as they would have been too heavy, so I would borrow a map from my host, and when I had walked off its edge, I would ask the next host to return it to the previous one and lend me the map of the next section. Sometimes if I did not have a map I would ask people the way. Strangely, people would try to direct me toward the main roads; when I said that main roads are not for walking on, that they are for cars and surely there must be a path for pedestrians, I would often discover that local people did not know their local footpaths. They would say: I wouldn't advise you to take the footpath—you will get lost; the paths are overgrown; it is much longer that way; or the farmer has plowed it up. But none of these answers would satisfy me, as I was prepared to make any amount of detour to avoid traffic, tarmac, fumes, and noise.

In fact I was much impressed by the number of long- and short-distance footpaths that exist in the English countryside. Three cheers for the National Trust, the Ramblers Association, and various other countryside conservers who fight and maintain these lovely paths! By being away from the main roads, I was much more intimately in the heart of Nature, without disturbance. On these rural paths I met the trees, animals, rocks, rivers, and birds, and realized the sacredness of all Nature. The churches, cathedrals, mosques and synagogues, shrines and temples are not the only holy places, but the whole of creation is divine and sacred. My pilgrimage was in every moment and in every place.

Sometimes I came across a tree which seemed like a Buddha or a Jesus: loving, compassionate, still, unambitious, enlightened, in eternal meditation, giving pleasure to a pilgrim, shade to a cow, berries to a bird, beauty to its surroundings, health to its neighbors, branches for the fire, leaves to the soil, asking nothing in return, in total harmony with the wind and the rain. How much I can learn from a tree! The tree is my church, the tree is my temple, the tree is my mantra, the tree is my poem and my prayer.

Standing under a tree by the Gapping River, I realized that the law of nature is to create energy and life by uniting. A seed united with the soil creates the tree; water united with the earth produces crops. When man and woman are united in love, they create a child. Wherever there is unity, sacred and positive energy is generated. How absurd that our modern materialistic mind is more accustomed to divide, to analyze, to split and separate. The extreme example of the splitting mind is the splitting of the atom. What do we get? Nuclear power and nuclear weapons: a grotesque manifestation of negative energy. When two become one, the third emerges. When the one is divided and fragmented, it brings destruction.

I had walked for about six hours, and as I was carrying no water I felt thirsty. When I saw a small farmhouse not far from the river Gapping, I left the path and walked across the field to it. I saw a woman in her late thirties, her hair bound up in a scarf, making the most of this rare sunny day the first of May. She was absorbed in gardening as if in meditation. I stood by the garden gate, slightly concerned that I should disturb her, but fortunately for me she happened to look over her shoulder, her face serene and smiling. Looking at her I forgot my thirst; there was a moment of suspense—neither of us knew why I was there. This moment passed, and she said "Hello." Gathering myself together I said, "I have been walking all day, the sun is hot, I am thirsty. Is it possible to get a glass of water?"

"Of course, do come in."

I followed her into the kitchen. "This man wants a glass of water," she said to her husband.

"Only a glass of water, or something stronger?"

"Anything, but not alcohol, would be fine."

"Cup of tea? Orange juice?"

"I would love a cup of tea."

"I would love one too," said the man, and offered me a chair by the long, pine table.

He was curious to know how far I had walked, why I was walking, and where I was walking to. When I told him that I had walked from Devon and was going to Lindisfarne and Iona and would be walking back through the mountains of north Wales, he said, "Rather you than me." But I could detect beneath his comment a little hint that he would also like to be free and on the road. When I told him that I was on a pilgrimage, he was even more intrigued. By the time I had told him snippets of my story and finished my cup of tea and homemade cake, he and his wife asked, "Why not stay for supper? Stay for the night?" I was touched. "It is very generous and kind of you to offer hospitality to a stranger like me."

"But we don't get a pilgrim walking around Britain every day. Stay and tell us more of your story."

However, I had already arranged to stay with a friend in Ipswich that evening, and therefore I had to apologize for not accepting their spontaneous invitation. Hospitality is alive and well in Suffolk, but unexpected guests are rare.

One of the important elements of my journey was a pilgrimage to people. I had arranged my itinerary in advance so that people would know when I was coming, so they could arrange a get-together of friends. I considered that those involved in care of the land, peace in the world, and regeneration of spiritual life were all holy people from whom I could take inspiration, and it was to them I journeyed.

———

Walking from Crowland via Spalding, I was making for Swineshead when suddenly a car stopped. As I passed by, the woman passenger asked if I would like a lift. I was deep in thought and never expected this offer. "Thank you for your kindness, but I am walking." "Where are you walking?" "To Swineshead." "We are also going to Swineshead. It will take you at least two hours to walk there, so why don't you get in the car, we will take you there."

At that moment, company would have been consoling and welcome, but I said: "You are very kind, but I must walk." The man said, "Just here people stand for hours showing their thumb and seeking a lift. Here we are offering you one, but if you don't want it, that's all right." They could not understand why I should refuse a lift and insist on walking. The man switched on the engine and was about to drive away. I quickly tried to explain that I was not trying to be rude or discourteous but that I was on a pilgrimage and had vowed to walk. The driver seemed unconvinced, and with a grumpy face he said, "OK, if that's what you want, good luck."

They drove off leaving me standing there, misunderstood. This I thought was the result of being on the road; looking again at my map, I discovered a dirt track leading toward Swineshead. I took it!

After about a mile a farmer came along on his tractor. "May I ask what you are doing here?" "I am making my way to Swineshead." "But you are trespassing on private land." "But this track is shown on the map and is not a dead end. Moreover I am harming no one and damaging nothing." "That is not the point; you are trespassing, and I don't want ramblers and hikers using my private land."

He was an example of some of the English country gentry who are extremely property-conscious. Offensive and ugly signs stating TRES-PASSERS WILL BE PROSECUTED; PRIVATE — KEEP OUT; GUARD DOGS PROTECT THIS PROPERTY; and BEWARE OF THE DOG are everywhere. I knew that there was no point in arguing, so I apologized. "I am very sorry, I didn't realize that this was a private track, but since I am already halfway along it, would you be kind enough to let me continue? I would be very grateful."

He was gracious enough to let me go.

At the point where the track joined a small country road stood the farmer's house, guarded by several Alsatian dogs. At some distance from the house they heard the sound of my footsteps and started barking loudly. With some nervousness I carried on, and as I came closer to the farm the dogs were frantic. On one side of the house there were two dogs chained, rushing up and down, straining to get at me but being jerked back by their chains. On the other side of the house a metal cage confined another two Alsatians trying hard, but unsuccessfully, to get out. They leapt up again and again at the bars of the cage, barking at the top of their lungs. My heart bled for these pathetic dogs. What has the farmer got that is so precious that he needs to imprison these poor dogs? This was not the only place where I experienced such a scene. People who whizz through cocooned in their cars may not realize it, but somebody who walks every day through the English countryside will experience the horror of farm after farm and house after house with imprisoned dogs to guard them.

The anger and ferocity of these dogs was a regular irritation in my walking experience.

————

York is a lovely city: the people have managed to keep out ugly modernization. Even the chain stores and department stores have been kept under control, with the old and the new standing side by side in harmony. It is usually a disappointment to come to big cities like Birmingham or Leeds—they don't look any different from one another. The same shops with the same goods, the same roads, the same houses, a monoculture of modernity that makes you wish you had stayed at home. Even as a stranger, I felt the friendliness of York's streets and houses and also the friendliness of those who dwell within them.

I stayed in St. Paul's Square, which is like a little hamlet or village: a community, closely knit together, everybody knowing each other, helping each other, and their children playing together on the open green of the square surrounded by magnificent trees towering above the tall houses. Although it is called a square, the houses in fact encircle the green. The roundness of the square makes it even more attractive, intimate, and homely. I remembered the American Indian Russell Means saying, "Roundness is equivalent to sacredness. The sun is round, the moon is round, the earth is round, the tree is round, the human body is round. Everything round is sacred." And I also remembered Ivan Illich saying, "You tell me where you live, and I'll tell you who you are." I wanted to tell Ivan that the people of York live in intimate squares like St. Paul's Square and they are very happy and human.

People were still talking about the lightning which had severely damaged a part of York Cathedral. Was it an act of protest on the part of the deity at the enthronement at York of David Jenkins, a man who disputes the Virgin Birth, as the bishop of Durham? Or was it a punishment to the church as a whole for discarding the principle of holy poverty? Or indeed both? Why did the lightning strike only the cathedral and nowhere else? It must have been an act of Providence. I heard the arguments with some amusement. What struck me was that the bishop of Durham was preferring history to myth. For myself I consider myth to be more capable than history of encompassing the complexity of truth. History is merely the accumulation of facts. Truth includes intuitive, experiential, and even irrational as well as rational aspects; fact is one aspect of the truth, but truth is greater than fact. How could a bishop be prepared to sacrifice truth to establish the facts? Apart from reflecting on this I could not offer any opinion on the act of the deity.

From York I came to the ruins of Fountains Abbey, which are well maintained by the National Trust, but more prettified than I would have liked them—presumably to please the tourists. The monks must have chosen this place for its wildness. By taming nature and turning it into a well-ordered park, some of the original magic of the place has been lost.

From Fountains Abbey I went to Rievaulx, and all my dreams of finding a ruined abbey in natural splendor were fulfilled. The ruins of Rievaulx stand in Rye Dale, a wooded valley of great power. Again the monks had chosen a magnificent site, and not an easy one. A canal was dug to connect the river Rye with the quarry so that stone for building the abbey could be brought to the exact spot, that most magical, inspirational, and holy place.

It is incredible to be in a monastery—built by human hands and with simple tools, and yet so ambitious a project. But in those days the monks were not obsessed with speed: they were not working for money, and the building of a monastery was an expression of their art, their craft, their livelihood, their dedication, and above all their good work in the service of the spirit. People told me that a lot of cheap labor was used, and the living conditions and the living standards of the workers were poor. But I couldn't help feeling that the quality of their life must have been good to produce such a monument of quality.

But of course when these abbeys and monasteries became centers of political power, and when material wealth and worldly possessions took precedence over spiritual seeking, their existence was threatened. The dissolution of the monasteries is not something over which I can shed any tears. Religion is an expression of the released spirit. When the Holy Ghost is imprisoned in monasteries, churches, temples, institutions, and disciplined orders, then it becomes frightening and haunting.

I walked along the river Rye and through Cropton Forest to Lastingham, to the crypt which was built by St. Ced of Lindisfarne fame. Thank goodness that St. Ced did not go for building great institutions like the abbeys of Fountains or Rievaulx but built a small church with a cavelike crypt conducive to meditation in the bleak surroundings of the Yorkshire moors. This crypt could not evoke envy; this small, simple space surrounded by stone walls embodies centuries of deep peace and eternal tranquillity—a perfect place to say the Peace Prayer.

I carried on through thick fog over the wild North Yorkshire moors. Neil, a student of architecture from Leeds, had joined me the previous day to walk from Fountains Abbey to Ampleforth. His intention had been to return home the same evening, but a day's walk had whetted his appetite. He asked my hosts, Otto and Rosemary Greenfield, if he could stay the night and walk on the next day.

As we walked over the wild North Yorkshire moors in the middle of May in thick fog, I was grateful that Neil had taken the decision to continue. Walking on my own would have been hair-raising. He said, "I love walking in the fog. I cannot see anything except the wet path under my feet, but I can imagine the rugged moorland around us. The fog is temporary. In a few hours, perhaps by evening or by tomorrow, it will be clear." I liked his relaxed, optimistic, and carefree attitude. There would have been no point in having someone complaining. He could easily have said, "How dreadful; we are only spending one day on this moor and it is

foggy." But he didn't, and we walked as much in the land of the imagination as we walked on the moor. We had very little idea whether we were
going north, east, or west. We believed that we were not going south since
that was where we were coming from, but apart from that, we were totally
in the lap of mist and mystery. The path was zigzagging and leading in all
directions, but we followed our noses. I said to Neil, "We don't want to get
lost on these moors, or our hosts tonight will be sending out helicopters in
search of lost pilgrims." But Neil was much more adventurous and without worry. He reassured me that it wouldn't come to that.

After about an hour, which seemed like ages, I was able to come to
terms with the fog, and I said to myself, "Whatever happens, we are in it,
so why worry?" There are times in life when you don't know where you are
and there is no alternative but to keep going in faith, trusting that in the
end everything will be all right. Sure enough, by the time we approached
the steep descent to Rosedale Abbey, the fog lifted and we could see the
magnificence of the moor all around us.

Our stop for that night, the twentieth of May, was at Botton Village, a
Camphill Community of the Steiner Movement. The village is spread
along the south-facing slopes of the valley, where approximately three
hundred people, the majority of them physically and mentally handicapped, live and work together. The community is divided into many
households, each with ten to fifteen handicapped members and two
houseparents. I stayed in one such minicommunity. I was much moved to
see all the members cooking together, eating together, cleaning together,
and supporting each other within the familylike environment of the
household. What a world of difference between institutions where handicapped people are dumped, looked down on, and seen as a burden to society, and this thriving village, where they are participants in the whole
range of daily activities and contribute a large percentage of the income.

I went to see the farm, the creamery, weaving, candle making, carpen-
try, glass engraving, printing, building, and numerous other activities
where handicapped and nonhandicapped were working side by side. I was

particularly inspired by a visit to the bakery, where the slowness of the handicapped bakers was no handicap at all. Rhythmic kneading of the dough by hand in a particular Steiner style was bringing everybody together. I could immediately feel that baking of bread for them was a sacred act. They were baking their daily bread for the whole Botton community as well as for a number of shops in the area. Baking bread as a source of healing the soul and feeding the body.

One of the members said to me, "If only people could learn to bake bread and share it with their family and neighbors, it would be a beginning of spiritual renewal in our society. We are what we eat. Bread is a staple and central part of our food. If we could bake bread with care and attention, our unhappiness, alienation, frustration, and bad relationships would diminish." This was a big claim. I looked into his face. "Are you sure?" "Yes, I am. I know what I am talking about and you can see it for yourself. Jesus Christ chose bread as the symbol of his own body—he could have chosen some other symbol, couldn't he? But he didn't, because bread is the real staff of life, and you cannot leave it to factories to make good wholesome bread for you."

I was impressed by his conviction. At home, my wife had always baked the bread. I decided that after the pilgrimage, when I returned home, I would begin to bake bread.

In the evening I was invited to speak about my journey to the residents of the village. I was warned that if any member of the audience should interrupt or distract me with noise or irrelevant questions, I should take no notice. When I stood in front of the packed hall, I was slightly hesitant and worried, but I started to speak in my normal way. As the story unfolded I could see beaming faces and eager eyes looking at me totally engaged. I spoke for an hour, and not once was I interrupted. Pure eyes and innocent faces in front of me with no trace of negativity, judgment, criticism, or skepticism made me feel that their handicap was only on the surface; their hearts are whole and souls unwounded. After my talk people were keen to come and thank me and shake my hands and invite me to their house. I was in tears with the warmth and love showered upon me. If these are the people whom we call handicapped, what is the word for the rest of us?

In the morning we climbed out of the valley and onto the moor again. Neil decided to walk with me for another day. We followed the Cleveland Way. The moorland here is rather boggy, so it was a great blessing to find this path studded with stepping-stones. I wondered how such beautifully shaped stones had been found—if they were brought here, it must have been a laborious task.

In the days of preindustrial Yorkshire, the people built beautiful stone walls, taking decades, sometimes generations, to turn their fields, farms, and landscapes into works of art. We make so much fuss about paintings, sculptures, and the art of building cathedrals, but people have unselfconsciously nurtured and cared for their land, their trees, and their paths in such a way that now, and for generations to come, we can enjoy the fruit of their work and find sustenance for our living. On my way to Guisborough the landscape itself appeared as a great painting. Old stone walls, with moss and lichen growing in them, but still firmly holding together, follow the shapes and curves of the hillsides. Fields are rounded and of different sizes. Standing on a viewpoint and gazing at the landscape was a fabulous feast for my eyes.

O Yorkshiremen and women of past generations, I thank you for leaving the land in such good heart and good shape. I hope that we also can leave the land in such a state that our children and grandchildren can be nourished by it.

Drunk with the beauty of the moor, Neil remembered the saying "Live as if you will die tomorrow, but farm as if you will live forever." The shepherds of Yorkshire still live through every stone, every wall, and every field.

Filled with feelings of awe, we reached the Beacon near Eston and from there looked down to see miles and miles of concrete and tarmac—the smoke-filled metropolis of Middlesborough and Billingham. What we humans do to the Earth! Yet the Earth is so tolerant, forbearing, and for-giving. Neil and I held our breath and, without much looking around, rushed through Middlesborough. The situation was much eased when a group of peace activists holding a welcome banner, met us on the bridge of the river Tees: they had organized a prayer meeting and reception for us in Billingham Church. We spent the night enjoying the warm hospitality of the minister of the United Reform Church and his wife.

I was not sorry to leave Billingham behind; I followed a disused railway line that had been converted to a footpath and cycle track. Although the path lasted for only a few miles, it was good to be on it, and when I left it I found myself in the midst of fields and woods. I was struck to see a herd of deer. I stopped walking and hid behind a hedge, curiously watching their swift movements. They were extremely alert and at once noticed my presence. I saw some kind of nervousness erupting, and they ran in all directions. One of them moved across the field like lightning and leaped over a high hedge. I was astounded by the sight of it. What energy! What suppleness! They live on grass and leaves alone—perhaps that is why they have such pure energy and innocence. Yes, innocence. When I was watching, before they ran away, I saw no sign of sin or ego in their eyes. They looked at me deeply, directly, and penetratingly. I saw some signs of confusion and perhaps fear, but that is all.

I arrived in the Durham of St. Cuthbert, a great Celtic saint. His remains are in the cathedral, and yet he lives in every corner of this splendid city. St. Cuthbert embodied the innocent divinity of a deer. He had no difficulty in communicating with birds, otters, and other members of the animal kingdom, as well as with human beings. He was a healer of wounded souls and a teacher of deep compassion.

Along the river Weir at Finchale Abbey, I saw a gypsy man who seemed to me an incarnation of St. Cuthbert. As I approached the abbey I was stopped by him for no apparent reason. "Where do you come from?" he asked with a tremendous force. "From Devon." "Now tell me the truth. Where do you come from?" "From India, then." "There you are. Where in India?" "Rajasthan." "There you are. The queen of Rajasthan is the world queen of all Romanies and gypsies. And as a gypsy, my people originate in Rajasthan. Now, hello, brother." He put out his hand to shake mine. "In my wagon I have rice and spices. Will you come and eat with me?" "It is very kind of you to invite me, but I must keep on the road. I have a date with people in Newcastle." "Never mind, next time. Tell all our people from Rajasthan that their brother lives here and has rice and spices for them." Then he opened the buttons of his jacket and showed a waistcoat which he claimed had been given to him by the queen of Rajasthan. "We gypsies believe that all boundaries, racial, national, or religious are fake. That is why we do not make boundaries and we do not live within boundaries, that is why we follow the free spirit. We will go where the wind leads us, we will go where the clouds lead us. All men are brothers, and all living creatures belong to the same family."

I heard his words, which were spoken with deep emotion, and could not help but conclude that St. Cuthbert would not have said anything very different. Walking in the land of St. Cuthbert, I felt he was accompanying me in spirit and showing me the way to Lindisfarne, which was only about one hundred miles away, five days' walk.

———

Battling along the north coast with the wind blowing in gusts of ninety miles an hour, I came at last to Lindisfarne, the Holy Isle, the Isle of St. Cuthbert. I arrived in time before the tide closed the causeway. I was in a sacred temple of which the sea is the keeper. Twice every day the sea opens the gates of the temple to let the pilgrims, the visitors, and even the tourists in. Tourists generally return before the sea closes the gates, but pilgrims are in no hurry. They stay the night or a few nights, to be soaked in the tranquillity and purity of the place. The monks who chose to build the priory here were very wise; there are very few such sacred sites where the sea is the guardian of the soul. The moment I stepped on the white sand I was free of the busy world. Here I was in the company of the sun, the sky, the sea, the sand dunes, and the spirits of saintly souls. St. Cuthbert prayed and meditated in solitude, totally surrendering himself to the sacred sound of the sea. Every night after midnight when all his fellow monks were asleep he would get up and go out. On one occasion, a curious monk, a light sleeper, noticed this and followed him. He found him in the sea up to his armpits, where he spent the night, occasionally singing hymns, and with only the waves for accompaniment. At daybreak Cuthbert came out of the sea and knelt on the sand to pray. Two otters followed in his footsteps, licked his feet, and warmed them with their bodies. This is the island where humans, nature, and religion are one.

The enchantment of being on this sacred island was further enhanced by the presence of my wife, June, and my children, Mukti and Maya, who had come to see me after two months' absence. I was making my pilgrimage by being away and June was making a pilgrimage by staying at home, taking responsibility for the house and the children, by herself. The longer I was away, the more I became aware that my voyage was only possible because June had stayed at home and released me: her letting go was a gift of love to me. I am deeply grateful to her for this. Leaving June, children, and Lindisfarne behind felt like traveling on without a ticket. But the Cheviots on my left and the Lammermuir Hills in front were like a gravitational force pulling me toward them.

SPIRITUAL DISCOMFORT

ate last March, I sat on the banks of the Ganges in Rishikesh, India, wondering if I should be in Kathmandu instead.

It's a delusion that occasionally seizes me on the road—the nagging anxiety that I've made a wrong turn, that I'm not where I should be, that the life I'm supposed to be living is waiting for me somewhere else, packaged and ready to go, like a take-out dinner I've ordered from a restaurant whose address I now can't remember.

For five months, I'd been traveling all over India doing research for a guidebook to ashrams and pilgrimage sites for spiritual tourists. Now it was almost time to head back to California, and to the routine grind of my job as an editor at *Yoga Journal.*

I wanted to finish my trip with a mystical adventure, and I had one in mind: a pilgrimage north up the sacred Ganges, worshiped by Hindus as a goddess incarnate, to its source at the ancient temple of Gangotri, high in the Himalayas. Fueling this vision was a phone call I'd gotten the week before I left for India from a close friend with lung cancer. "I had a dream that you were supposed to bring me some air from Gangotri," he had told me. "Just take a deep breath and hold it till you get back."

But after three days in Rishikesh, the launching pad for the Gangotri pilgrimage made by tens of thousands of Hindus every summer, I was reluctantly facing the fact that my timing was off.

I needed to be back in Delhi within two weeks, to catch my flight to California. But the road to Gangotri, I learned in Rishikesh, was buried by landslides and avalanches thirty-seven miles short of the holy temple, which was still closed for the winter.

And although a trekking agent I consulted assured me that I could hike there cross-country, "no problem," the expedition he described was an eight-day, subfreezing trek through unplowed snowdrifts—hauling camping gear handed down from the Indian army, circa 1965—with only a hired guide for company. "No problem," the agent assured me again. "Our guide is very good chap, speaking some English, will be discussing with you philosophy of life and all like that." That clinched it. I resigned myself to remaining in the foothills.

For any reasonable person, Rishikesh would be sufficiently magical. It's the "gateway to the gods," a holy pilgrimage spot, where the Ganges descends from the Himalayas to the plains. The river rushed at my feet, bottle-green over glinting white boulders. I gazed across the water at a pastel froth of spired and turreted temples and ashrams, peach and pink and yellow and baby blue—I'd never seen a city that so strongly resembled a six-year-old's birthday cake.

The streets were jammed with pilgrims, from the wandering ascetics known as sadhus, whose painted faces and tridents marked their allegiance to Shiva, the god of destruction, to a gang of blonde yoga students in immaculate white *kurtas*, arguing heatedly in German. A rubber raft floated by, bearing a load of tipsy white-water rafters in life jackets and helmets, belting out the theme song from a popular Hindi film.

But none of it charmed me—I was too distracted by the foul weather inside my head. My mind felt hard and lumpy, like a bed that I couldn't get comfortable in, no matter how hard I tried.

Rishikesh seemed like a spiritual Disneyland, mysticism packaged for tourists. I yearned for the raw, wild spirit of the Himalayas, where solitary yogis spend decades in mountain caves, practicing ascetic rites to get closer to God.

I was tired of doing things alone but also tired of meeting new people—after five months on the road, I was sick of being the new kid in town every single week. I wanted to find someone to go to Gangotri with me, but it's a tough way to initiate conversation by saying, "Would you like to go on a long and grueling hike through the snow with me? We really need to leave tomorrow, since I don't have much time . . ."

This is about as effective as announcing, five minutes into a first date, that you're only interested in a committed monogamous relationship and you want to have a baby within a year.

Two days later, the travel gods came to my rescue. I met a traveling companion, a thirty-seven-year-old Spanish spiritual seeker named Maria. Maria didn't want to go all the way to Gangotri, but she was heading halfway there, up the river to an ashram near Uttarkashi, where she'd heard an enlightened guru was in residence. I rented a sleeping bag from the trekking agent—its approximate weight was 235 pounds, but I was sure the lead lining would prove very useful in the event of nuclear attack. I strapped it to my backpack, determined that if I couldn't make it to Gangotri, I'd at least get as close as I could.

Maria and I wedged ourselves—along with six chain-smoking men—into a 1950s-model Ambassador taxi, which blasted north along twisting mountain roads. The driver's strategy for negotiating hairpin turns was to barrel around them as quickly as possible, so as to minimize the time spent in the danger zone. (He was only egged on by poetic roadside signs like "Life's a Journey—Let's Finish It" and "Corner Cutters Drop Dead Into Gutters.") When I dared open my eyes, though, the drive was spectacular—terraced green valleys, rugged hills thick with birch and pine, and, snaking along below us, the silver ribbon of the Bhagirathi River, one of the two strands that come together to form the Ganges. As we climbed higher and higher, snow-tipped peaks began poking up in the distance, then vanishing again, in a kind of striptease hint of pleasures to come.

Ten minutes after Maria and I arrived in Uttarkashi (a sudden snarl of traffic, temples, and shops, lodged in a bend in the river) we met a wilderness guide drinking *chai* at the Belur Hotel. He was a gentle, somber man named Jai Singh, who taught at a local mountaineering school. Jai Singh informed me that the information I had gotten in Rishikesh was incorrect. (This wasn't surprising—information in India is composed more of rumors than facts, and the truth must be arrived at by carefully comparing multiple versions of the same story, like a scholar analyzing Biblical texts.) The road was open as far as Hirsil, twelve miles from Gangotri, he assured me. From there, we could hike to Gangotri in a single day.

Maybe I'd been drinking too much *chai*. In a burst of caffeinated enthusiasm, I hired him.

The next morning, I left Maria to explore the joys of a new guru, and with Jai Singh as my guide, I scrambled into a bus heading north and up. We drove to where the road was blocked by an avalanche, at an altitude of about nine thousand feet. Then I hoisted my backpack and began to hike.

Aside from an occasional rock slide or avalanche, the path was clear; the climb was steady but gradual. When the pilgrimage season opened, Jai Singh explained, the road would be roaring with buses and jeeps, delivering loads of pilgrims, boom box–toting picnickers, and Western backpackers. But now it was blissfully deserted. Until the paved road was built in the 1960s—as a military response to tensions with China—the only way to get to Gangotri from Rishikesh had been on foot. I was grateful that I was getting a taste of the original flavor of this pilgrimage.

The only other pilgrims we passed were a few solitary sadhus, tramping along in ragged robes and sandals. In India there are millions of sadhus, wandering ascetics whose path of renunciation has been an integral part of India's social and spiritual fabric for over three thousand years. Living on alms—and traditionally forbidden to stay in any one place for longer than three days—most of them wander from holy site to holy site, practicing ascetic rites and rituals designed to break their attachment to the world and bring about blissful union with God. Others live in solitude in remote mountain forests and caves. Many modern Indians complain that most of these "holy men" are simply beggars in orange robes—what I'd come to call pseudo-sadhus. But few will risk offending a genuine saint by refusing alms.

Snowy Himalayan peaks soared ahead of us to over twenty thousand feet. The slopes around us were thick with blue pine, rhododendrons, oak, and horse chestnuts. We stopped at a mud shack for *chai* boiled over a wood fire, tasting of smoke and cardamom. As we approached Gangotri, we began to pass seedy clumps of deserted tourist bungalows, covered up to their windowsills in dirty snow banks. In a few weeks, Jai Singh told me, tourist buses would be bumper to bumper for two miles ahead of Gangotri.

Finally, just as my ankles were starting to ache, we arrived at Gangotri itself, at 10,300 feet: a fantastically beautiful jumble of water-sculpted, caramel-colored granite, with the pale green river seething through it, and a fantastically ugly jumble of tourist hotels, growing on the banks in a giant fungus of cinder block and brick—many of them still half built, with bristles of rebar protruding from their unfinished walls like punk hairdos. In the middle of them stood the ancient temple to the goddess Ganga, a squat stone cube painted sky blue and silver, sealed off with an iron grating until the opening ceremonies, three weeks away.

We paused below the temple at the bathing ghat that marked the place where King Bhagirathi had meditated for thousands of years, begging the Ganga to descend from heaven to purify the sins of his ancestors. As we dipped our fingertips respectfully in the icy water, we were greeted by a raisin-faced swami in an orange robe and orange slippers—even his two remaining teeth looked a bit orange. He escorted us to his rough stone shack, where he fixed us a heaping plate of rice and *dahl* and cup after cup of ultra-sweet *chai*, laced with ginger and pepper.

We spent the night in Danda Swami's shack, with snow falling outside and the wind hissing through the cracks of the wooden shutters. The carpet was burlap bags, the ceiling was a plastic tarp, the toilet was a snow bank fifty feet away. I was wildly happy. Finally, I thought smugly, I was on my way to a real adventure.

However, I wasn't yet at the true source of the Ganges. Over the centuries, the glacier has retreated from Gangotri, and now the actual spot where the water gushes forth from the ice is at Gomukh—the "Cow's Mouth"—another twelve miles of steep climbing on an unpaved trail. The trail to Gomukh was reportedly still impassable, but Jai Singh thought we might be able to make it through. He recommended that we take an exploratory day hike in that direction, to see what the conditions were like—leaving our backpacks, food, and sleeping bags in Gangotri. Our aim was to make it as far as Chirbasa, an evergreen grove in a valley halfway between Gangotri and Gomukh, before turning around and returning to our lodge in Gangotri to spend the night.

The trail was steep and narrow, slicing along the edge of precipitous hillsides and cliffs above the Bhagirati. It was occasionally covered in snow or buried by a rock slide or avalanche, and I was glad I wasn't carrying a pack as I picked and scrambled my way along. The sleek white slopes were broken by groves of *deodar* and *bhujbas*—a member of the beech family, on whose papery bark the great Indian epic called the *Mahabarata* is said to have first been written down. The sky was pigeon-gray, the peaks toward Gomukh were draped in clouds, and the wind bit at my bare neck. But the climbing kept me warm, even in my windbreaker and light cotton pants, and I figured Jai Singh would steer us back if the weather got too threatening.

Not far from Gangotri, we passed a boulder that sported the spray-painted slogan "Holy man 400 mtrs. Ask any questions"—with a wobbly arrow pointing down toward the riverbed. "Is there a sadhu living there?" I asked.

"Summertime only," Jai Singh answered. "Summertime, so many sadhus coming, painting their faces, wearing robes and *malas*, getting so much money from so many tourists. Wintertime, going to Uttarkashi, going to Delhi, living in house with central heat, watching BBC, MTV, Star TV."

"How many of the sadhus we see are real sadhus?" I asked.

He thought for a minute, then answered, "Maybe 8 percent, 10 percent maximum."

Jai Singh's idea of a day hike was a little different from mine. Chirbasa, it turned out, was a good seven miles from Gangotri, at an altitude of close to thirteen thousand feet. By the time we sighted its cluster of pines, dark against the snowy slopes, my legs were aching, my breath was shallow and quick, and I was sincerely regretting having brought along nothing to eat but half a Cadbury chocolate bar. "Half an hour more," Jai Singh said cheerfully. "One hour, maximum—" and suddenly the wind began to blow hard down the valley. Within minutes we were wrapped in swirling snowflakes so thick we couldn't see Chirbasa at all.

We stopped and looked at each other. "Blizzard," Jai Singh announced.

"Should we turn around?"

"Going back is not so good. Can't see trail, can't see cliffs. Could be some avalanche coming."

"Then what do we do?"

"We go on to Chirbasa. There is one *baba* staying there in a cave. We can spend the night with him, if he is having some blankets."

A surge of anticipation wiped out my anxiety. Food, camping gear, warm clothes—what did they matter, really, if finally, after months of pseudo-sadhus, I would meet . . .

"Is this one a pretend sadhu?" I asked.

"He is the real thing," said Jai Singh.

But when we made our way into Chirbasa, slipping and stumbling on hidden boulders as the trail fast disappeared under fresh snow, it wasn't a sadhu we encountered first. Instead, the tableau that appeared amid the swirling flakes was a tall, gray-haired man in a full-body Goretex snowsuit, accompanied by a porter and a guide, sitting by a campfire next to a brilliant orange dome tent. Water was boiling and the porter was arranging chocolate cookies on a metal tray. The whole scene looked like a Christmas-season TV spot for REI.

"I do hope you're not from L.A.," the gray-haired man greeted me in a *Masterpiece Theatre* accent. "People from L.A. are such total stinkers."

"San Francisco," I clarified.

"Oh, that's a tad better. As long as you're not into any of those spiritual fads, you can stay for tea."

I looked at the cookies, the bubbling *chai*. I know when to keep my mouth shut. I resolved that if pressed, I would tell him I worked for *Plumber's Journal*.

The man's name was Menno; he was an advertising producer from London. He'd been trying to make it to Gomukh but had been forced to turn back; even with ice pick, snow boots, and full winter gear, the trail had proved too difficult, with neck-deep snow and the threat of landslides and avalanches. "Last night, " he lamented, "I had to wipe my bum with snow."

"That wasn't a positive experience?" I asked. "You don't want to re-create it at home, with an ice chest next to your toilet?"

"It would have been all right if it had been a two-minute crap," he said morosely. "This one went on for hours."

I rubbed the crumbs from my mouth and looked at Jai Singh. "Maybe," I suggested, "we should go looking for that *baba* soon?"

The sadhu lived in a cave on a ledge high on a snow-draped hillside, with a tiny lean-to of stone and plastic tarps attached to the cave's mouth. Roused from meditation by Jai Singh—who called *"Maharaj! Jai, Maharaj!"* and flashed my feeble, dying Maglite around the inside of the lean-to—he drew back the canvas flap of the door and stood squinting at us in the snow-reflected light. He was a thin man, apparently in his fifties or sixties, with a twisted knot of black beard and a great mass of hair bundled up in a brown scarf. He did not seem entirely pleased to see us on his doorstep.

Vehement talking in Hindi followed, along with much gesticulation toward me and an occasional phrase in English from Jai Singh, who appeared to be listing the credentials that made me worth rescuing from the storm: "Journalist . . . yoga . . . pure vegetarian."

Finally, a deal was struck. We were welcome to stay with the sadhu, if we didn't mind sleeping on the bare dirt floor of his storeroom, with one thin blanket as our only bedding and no fire. But the sadhu ate only one meal a day—consisting mainly of nuts and potatoes—and he'd already had it. So if we wanted dinner, we'd have to beg it from Menno.

We plowed through the mounting drifts back to Menno's campsite, a journey that felt like a snowy form of time travel—could Menno and the *Maharaj* possibly coexist in the same century? I hung my soaked socks to dry by the fire and sat as close to the flames as I could without igniting, watching the steam rise from my damp cotton pants. Menno boiled up a pot of Top Ramen—"Macho Masala," a flavor I've never encountered in California—and regaled me with stories of drinking binges in London, Las Vegas, Amsterdam, and Los Angeles. ("And so there I was, locked out of my apartment in Soho; and so I wobbled on down to the local police station and slurred, 'Excuse me, officer, I've misplaced my keys; would you mind putting me up in an empty cell for the night? My firm will be happy to make you an appropriate donation.' And they were just about to give me a bed when word came in on the radio that there had just been a drug raid, and they were bringing in twenty-five new criminals for the night, so I couldn't have a cell. I tell you, I made a stinking fuss. 'What about me?' I was almost crying. 'What about the cell you promised me?'")

By the time we made it back to the sadhu's cave, it was almost dark and still snowing hard. We pushed in through the canvas door flap and shone my Maglite around. We were in a tiny, dirt-floored room, with walls of misfitting stones with burlap and plastic tarps stretched over the gaps, a roof of birch poles supporting more burlap and plastic tarps, and plenty of gaps everywhere for frigid air to circulate. Hanging from the ceiling were woven baskets, piled with cloth sacks of potatoes. Behind the canvas-draped door that led to the entrance of the cave itself, we could hear the sadhu chanting in occasionally faltering Sanskrit.

Tentatively, I pulled aside the flap and peeked inside: our host was sitting cross-legged next to an oil lamp, peering at yellowing manuscript pages through Buddy Holly spectacles. He did not look up at my intrusion. Dropping the flap, I pulled a blanket around me and sat down to meditate. For half an hour I tried to focus on my breath and the Sanskrit song, which contained a recurring phrase I recognized from my days as an undergraduate religion major: *"Neti, neti . . ."* "Not this, not this." It is from the transcendent vision of the Upanishads, the mystical verses composed three thousand years ago by seers in deep meditation: "Is this body the true Self? No, not this. Are the thoughts the true Self? No, not this. The feelings? No, not this . . ."

When I opened my eyes, Jai Singh was looking at me. "While you were meditating," he said brightly, "three very large rats ran next to you. Back and forth, back and forth. Oh, very, very large!"

For the first time, my enthusiasm began to falter. I'd been feeling pretty excited about the chance to spend one night as an honest-to-God ascetic. But rats?

A few minutes later, the sadhu pulled aside the flap and stuck his head into our chamber. Through Jai Singh, I asked him his name, which he said was Rampal; he had been living in this cave for fifteen years, he said, ever since Gangotri had begun to feel too social for a serious sadhu.

Rampal began to lecture me sternly in Hindi, which Jai Singh translated. If I ate mutton, he informed me, I would have to spend sixty-four lifetimes as an animal before attaining human birth again. I assured him that I didn't eat mutton (but I thought, a little guiltily, of the occasional sushi—how many lifetimes for a piece of *maguro?*). "This human life is precious," Rampal told me. "So rare it is, to be born a human! Do not waste your time."

Abruptly, the interview was over. Rampal dropped the curtain and retreated into his cozy chamber—the really luxurious part of the cave, where there was even a fire flickering. As a woman and a foreigner, Jai Singh explained, I would pollute his home by entering and necessitate several lifetimes of penances.

My mini-Maglite was barely functioning, casting a faint circle of light about as big as a quarter. From the bottom of my day pack I pulled out a stub of candle, left over from some ashram ritual months ago. "Do you have any matches?" I asked my wilderness guide, hopefully. "Madam," he replied with stern indignation, "I am not a smoker."

A few minutes later, my light blinked out, and I lay down on a floor as cold as an ice-skating rink, huddled under a rat-gnawed blanket. In the next room, I could hear Rampal chanting the lilting song that accompanies *arati*, the ritual "offering of fire." I peeked though his flap and watched him swirling a candle flame in a circle before his altar. Then I watched as, still chanting the name of Ram, he busied himself in another ceremony involving a flickering flame and a kettle: it took me a while to realize that he was preparing a pot of tea. Wistfully, I dropped the flap and prepared to shiver my way through the night.

Every half hour or so, I'd hear the thunder of an avalanche cascading from a nearby peak. With every crash, Rampal would toss in his bed on the other side of the curtain and call out praises to the gods—"*Jai,* Sita, Ram!" To keep myself warm, I tried to practice the yogic breathing technique known as "breath of fire," a vigorous bellows-like snort that, after all, had probably been developed in a cave much like this one. Using such practices, some yogis can raise their body temperatures high enough to dry wet blankets in subzero temperatures. I soon discovered that I am not one of them. Instead I settled for turning over every fifteen minutes, whenever the part of me pressed against the floor started to go numb.

I was starting to get tired of my adventure. All right, I'd visited an actual sadhu in his cave; I'd had my sampling of genuine mystical experience. Now could we fast-forward the tape to the time when I'd be back in

Rishikesh, drinking *lassi* by the Ganges again? How had I failed to appreciate its charms? My bones were aching, my nose was running, my head throbbed with exhaustion and the effects of the high altitude. I'd been waiting for weeks for a mystical moment; now that it was here, I couldn't wait for it to be over.

The most exotic experience, I reflected, is made up of the most mundane details. I was in a Himalayan cave with a holy man; back in California, I could tell that to my yogi friends and they'd moan with envy. Yet the actual experience mainly consisted of damp socks, numb fingers, sore throat, and shivering jaw. Maybe my spiritual teachers were right when they told me, over and over, that all moments are equally magical, if we give them our full attention. Maybe my mystical adventure had been happening all along. Maybe Menno was as mysterious as Rampal.

I wondered if Rampal found his own life extraordinary—alone year-round, with nothing to do but meditate, chant, study scripture, and pray. Was he happy? Did he manage to attain—at least intermittently—the state of blissful union with the cosmos that is the ultimate goal of a yogi's practice?

Another wall of snow crashed from a distant mountain. *"Jai,* Sita, Ram!" called Rampal. *"Jai,* Sita, Ram," I whispered, and turned my other side to the icy floor.

Toward dawn, Rampal began to sing again. I peeked into his chamber and watched his shadowy figure moving about his cave, singing in Sanskrit, the ancient language whose syllables yogis believe have the power to shape reality. As pale light began to seep in between the chinks in our stone walls, Jai Singh lifted our canvas door flap and we peered out at huge drifts of snow, with scattered flakes still falling.

Rampal poked his head out and began speaking urgently to Jai Singh. "He says we must go now," Jai Singh translated. "More snow will be coming. Avalanches could also be coming as day is getting warmer. If we stay, could be trapped here long time." Clearly, this thought was as alarming to Rampal as it was to me.

I pulled on my boots; Jai Singh wrapped his feet in plastic bags and slid them into his canvas tennis shoes. We stepped out into the drifts, put our hands in the prayer position, bowed to our host, and started off.

But before we left, I took a long look out over the valley, blanketed in snow, with the dark thread of the river snaking through it and the mountain peaks disappearing into clouds. I thought of my friend who had asked me to bring him some Gangotri air—and I took a deep breath, and held it.

JAPANESE PILGRIMAGE

I failed and the failure still weighs on me. . . .

It happens shortly after we leave the temple, the bangai, where Kobo Daishi is said to have been schooled as a boy—on that bright spring day made gay by the temple festival, after hospitality had been lavished on us in the setting of the temple garden. The priest comes to the entry to see us off and points out a path leading straight down to the highway, the shortest way to the next temple. We dislike walking along highways but it is growing late and we know we must hurry to reach before dark the temple where we have made a reservation for the night.

Just before we reach the highway there is a cluster of new houses. A woman emerges from one of them and invites us in for a cup of tea as settai. We have been drinking tea for the past hour and are pressed for time but this is not the kind of invitation one can refuse. In the entryway she invites us into her home but we beg off, asking if we may just sit here without shedding our shoes. She brings us coffee, which is a treat, and chats with us sociably as we enjoy it. From within I hear a hum of voices, almost a monologue, the solemn, didactic tone of a man delivering a disquisition, only occasionally broken as a young woman assents.

We start to thank our hostess and go our way when she asks if we will come in to meet her family. Please, won't we come into the living room?

I assume she wants us to admire her children, perhaps to give them the chance to say they met a foreigner, but Morikawa and I both know that once we enter we cannot break away quickly. We make excuses—it will soon be dark and we have a long way to go.

Now she bares what is on her mind. She focuses on me. Will I, she begs, examine her daughter, who is suffering from a chest condition? The urgency in her tone, the sound of the voices from within—I have the feeling that the illness is serious.

I know what this woman is asking. Just this morning we encountered a healer. Morikawa spotted a sign saying that a couple of hundred yards off our road was "a temple related to Kobo Daishi." Curiosity took us there, a small chapel adjoining a house. A woman answered the door, a priestess. Over tea and cookies she sketched the chapel's brief history: it was opened by an aged nun who settled here after making the pilgrimage; when she died an elderly priest came from the city to live out his life here; then it was taken over by two nuns "who were unsuccessful"; when they moved on about three years ago this woman came, after (like that first nun) completing the pilgrimage. What was it, I wondered, that she was evidently successful at but the two nuns were not. She told us: "People suffering from illnesses, physical and mental, come and ask me to perform rituals of prayer for them." She was a shaman, a healer.

Now I am asked to be one. As a man with hair gray enough to imply some wisdom; as a stranger—there is mystery in that word, the mystery of a person unknown unexpectedly appearing from a world unknown—and doubly a stranger, a foreigner; and above all as a *henro,* I am being asked to minister to a sick girl.

I panic, utterly at a loss. Nothing I have studied has prepared me for this. Suddenly I am not a *henro,* I am a misplaced doctor's son from Illinois (one who instinctively shied away from his father's profession). I have no religious power, I tell this woman. I am wearing a *henro* robe but I have no religious power. I have no ability to diagnose an illness or to cure it.

She pleads with me just to look at her daughter. Another daughter, an attractive young woman, comes to the entry, kneels, and smiling, joins her mother in urging us in.

I repeat that there is nothing I can do for the girl, that I am afraid anything I might do would only make things worse. I urge them to call a doctor.

I try to explain, to justify. It's not that I don't want to help, I say, it's that I can't. I have no power, no competence. Morikawa I know is as agonized as I am. He is caught between these pleading women and his demoralized companion. Full of apologies, we make our escape.

We plod along the highway, single file for safety's sake. There is no chance to talk. I am shaken. I feel painfully inadequate. Why didn't I ask Morikawa what to do instead of showering him with a torrent of excuses to interpret? What should I have done? I know only that I have failed.

The fates are not slow to punish me, and Morikawa because he is with me. Darkness overtakes us. We phone to find that because we are so late there is no room for us at the temple. (We have violated a cardinal precept of the Exhortation, "the rule of setting out early and putting up early. . . . If one tries to go on a little farther, the way often stretches out; before one realizes it, it is late and one does not know where to stay.") We end up at an unpleasant inn where we are served an unpalatable meal, which (that and weariness and failure) promptly makes me ill.

Several days later we come across another of Tosa's articles about his pilgrimage and I learn what I should have done. With his permission I quote; he speaks of himself in the third person.

The scene is of thatch-roofed farmhouses and peach trees in full bloom. A lone pilgrim, weary, his white robe soiled, walks with dragging feet, trying to keep his eyes on the blossoms. He hears someone calling him:

"O-henro-san!" He turns to see an old lady running after him and he stops to wait. When she reaches him, all out of breath, she offers tea at her house. He is thirsty and he thinks it will not take much time. "It's very kind of you," she answers, and follows her back.

It turns out to be quite a distance, but remembering how she had run after him he puts down any temptation to refuse and continue on his way. Finally she points out one of the thatched houses. Like the others it has a peach tree blooming in its garden.

He sits on the veranda, she serves tea and cakes, and they chat. Suddenly the old lady straightens and becomes formal. "O-henro-san, will you do me a favor? I have a granddaughter who is eighteen years old. She has been sick in bed for a long time. Will you pray at her bedside to charm away her illness?"

The henro is astonished by this unexpected request but he realizes that it is a serious matter. He tells her, "I can pray but I am not Kobo Daishi. I too am seeking the Daishi's help. I am just one of many henro."

Earnestly she says, "That is enough. What I ask is that you pass your album over her sick body."

Now the henro remembers that when he was a child, every time he had a stomachache or a fever his grandmother would pass a thick book over him while she repeated, "You will get better soon; you will get better soon." The book was the album of her pilgrimage to the Eighty-eight Sacred Places of Shikoku. She treasured it and when she died it was buried with her. This comes back to him very clearly now and he nods in assent.

She is gratified, and leading him into the house she shows him to the room where her granddaughter lies. Her bed is by the window so that she can look at the peach blossoms. The old woman speaks lovingly to the girl, who silently turns her face to the henro. It is clear, unclouded. She smiles and greets him with her wide eyes. He looks into them, at a loss for words.

He hears the grandmother explain . . . when the girl was nine years old she was attacked by tuberculosis of the spine . . . she was taken to doctor after doctor but it was no use . . . since then she has lain in bed.

It is her pure eyes that hold the henro. Then she speaks: "I'm sorry to trouble you. I suppose my grandmother asked you in. I keep telling her that we should not interrupt henro because they are in a hurry."

Her voice is bright and it banishes the depression he has felt. He finds it easy to talk now. He introduces himself and tells her where he's from. She listens alertly and sometimes she asks questions. In a short time they are talking freely.

"I have made more than a hundred friends among henro." She pauses and then she confides, "When I become dejected I turn the pages of my diary and try to remember each of them. I'm so grateful to them. And now, will you pray with your new album?"

He hands her his album in its cover of golden brocade. Her eyes shine. "Albums get more gorgeous every year. This is wonderful." She puts it on her young breasts and closes her eyes. His heart overflows and he prays silently, afraid to trust his voice. He sees something he should not: a tear flows gently, gently down her cheek.

Along the same stretch of road where the girl's grandmother hailed Tosa, Morikawa and I catch up with a lone henro and walk with him as far as the bus stop he is heading for. "Two years ago I made half the pilgrimage," he tells us. "Now I want to complete it. . . . My reasons? Well, my grandson has heart disease—he's just a little fellow, only six years old—and I pray for his recovery. I'm not in good health myself: there's a hole in my heart. And I have a neighbor who is mongoloid. I say prayers for my grandson, my neighbor, and myself."

There are literally numberless stories of cures wrought by the Daishi, of the blind given sight, of the crippled enabled to stand and walk. One hears of such miracles at every temple and along the path between. Several temples have collections of casts and braces and crutches left by those who no longer needed them.

The doors of temples are crowded with written supplications: for a sick child, often with a photo that gives my heart a wrench; for better sight or hearing—sheets filled with a single character for "eye" or "ear." There is a chapel—unnumbered, a bangai—whose deity specializes in diseases of the breast; its walls are covered with replicas of breasts brought by women who prayed there. At several temples there are altars enshrining a god, more Shinto than Buddhist, whose province is woman's anatomy "from the waist down." "It was holy men who installed that god here," says one priest; "its altar had two or three centuries of prosperity but almost no one visits it anymore." Yet some temples report that it is popular with women of the entertainment quarters who come to seek protection from venereal disease, and others that it is visited by women who suffer ill health after giving birth. As for birth, I have not been able to count the temples with deities noted for their power to grant pregnancy and easy delivery; the sheer number of such altars speaks eloquently of the life that Japanese women have lived—the obligation to bear children, the perils of childbirth in the past. Temple Sixty-one has in two generations changed from the poorest to the richest among the eighty-eight based largely on a single premise: that prayers and guidance there will enable a childless couple to have a child. It seems evident that for many Japanese medical science needs all the help it can get, if indeed it is the remedy of choice.

I do not mean to belittle the importance of state of mind. Though it is difficult for me to believe that the pilgrimage can cure cancer—we encounter a few henro who say that is what they are praying for—I know that there are diseases it can cure. Polio or a stroke, for example: if the victim can walk at all, then the hard physical exercise (some would call it therapy) and the getting out into nature (for nature has therapeutic powers), if accompanied by faith, can work miracles—but not without faith.

A priest at one of the temples has told me: "In the old days many who were ill made the pilgrimage; lepers, for instance, were numerous along the henro-path. Nowadays the physically ill go to hospitals. But these are times of strain and mental illness, and so today the benefits of pilgrimage are greater than ever."

The young Shingon priest I traveled with on my first pilgrimage was named Mizuno. Late one day we found ourselves in the river valley between Temples Twenty and Twenty-one. It had been a hard day: down from one height and a long walk before we climbed to Twenty and then lurched and stumbled (I speak of myself; he was surer-footed) down its mountain. There we faced the forbidding form of the mountain on which Twenty-one stands. Night was coming on and we were all in. There is a village in the valley by the river and we asked if there was a house that lodged henro. There was; we found it and were taken in.

Shortly after we arrived a couple appeared, a man and wife whom I guessed to be in their sixties. They were shown to a room upstairs, we being downstairs, but when it came time for supper the housewife called them down to eat with us. And so it was I heard their story.

They introduced themselves as Mr. and Mrs. Ishii from Okayama City, across the Inland Sea. They owned a small apartment building, they said, but they were not really city folk; they had been farmers until they had to sell their land because Mrs. Ishii's health was so poor that she could no longer do her share of the work. For twenty years or more she had suffered from a nervous ailment: headaches, sleeplessness, malaise, her condition becoming progressively worse. She lost weight: "I looked like a ghost." They went to physician after physician; each ended by saying he could do nothing for her.

They explained that for years they had been worshipers of Kobo Daishi. Their farming village had had no temple and they had joined with their neighbors to form one, of the Shingon sect.

"About a year ago," Mr. Ishii continued, "my wife's health was so bad and worsening so fast that we had just about given up"—I got the impression that they had contemplated suicide together, though they certainly didn't say so. As a last resort, they decided to undertake the pilgrimage.

"We realized that she might die attempting it," Mr. Ishii said, "but no other hope was left to us."

They started at Number One. For several days it was agonizing for her, and for him at her side. They were able to walk only a short distance each day but they went as far as they could, and they prayed, they prayed. Slowly she began to gain strength; the days became a little easier. They went all the way around and by the time they reached Temple Eighty-eight she was in truth cured.

A year later, as we sat there at supper, her weight was normal, her color was good, and she looked fit. I told her so and she demurred a little: "I'm not completely well. But I can live again. Each morning and evening I pray in gratitude to Kobo Daishi." Mr. Ishii finished: "We have returned to give thanks. We don't do all the pilgrimage—only Awa—but every year for the rest of our lives we intend to do at least one province." (There is a tradition of doing Shikoku's four provinces one at a time, with an interval between.) "We cannot forget that we have been blessed."

I went to bed conscious that I had heard the story of a miracle. I knew that the regimen of the pilgrimage had been vital—the physical exercise, the closeness to nature, and just getting away from home; but without faith they would not have been enough. I have thought of the Ishiis often in the years since. I hope that spring still brings them back as henro to worship in thanksgiving.

It was the next day, on that first pilgrimage, that we fell in with a young henro. I had glimpsed him first at Temple Twenty. A slight, pale young man with long hair, he stood out among the elderly. We met again at Temple Twenty-two. It was noon, and the young priest and I had improvidently neglected to provide ourselves with lunch. He offered us a box lunch, saying he had an extra one, and the two of us shared it.

I wondered why a young man would set out alone on the pilgrimage. He was a little shy and he volunteered nothing but he did not seem to mind my questions. He came originally from a town in northern Japan, in the "snow country." Of his family he said that they did "nothing much";

no, they were not farmers. He was the second of three sons. At fifteen, as soon as he had finished junior high school and the years of compulsory education, he left home for Tokyo. With little to offer in skills or experience, he found a job in a potato chip factory. I looked at his hands: they were slender and soft.

As is usual, the shop provided a dormitory for its workers: he and about thirty others lived in a loft above the factory. Each had a low-ceilinged cubicle about six by nine. I asked about recreation. Nothing, he said, but television and once in a while a movie. He worked six long days a week.

He was twenty-four. After nine years of working in a small factory for small wages, of a life that was leading nowhere, he was fed up. He said he was having "personal problems"; I took that to mean friction with his boss and co-workers, a suffocating sense of futility, and perhaps the onset of a nervous breakdown.

He had been given few holidays; now he was taking one for himself. He had quit his job and set out on the pilgrimage. "People in Tokyo said I'd find Shikoku dead, but I like it here." I asked his purpose; he said he had none. Obviously he was bent on escape from a life that was strangling him, but he was not running aimlessly: he was seriously engaged in the pilgrimage. Unlike the few other young people we saw, he wore the henro's white robe, a bell hung from his waist, and he was earnest in performing the rituals at the temples.

He was making the pilgrimage with no time schedule and no deadline; he said he would take as long as he wished. I sensed that he was hungry for companionship but our schedules did not mesh. We drifted apart at Temple Twenty-three. When I last saw him he was praying ardently before the main hall. I hope his pilgrimage brought him what he was looking for, someone or something to give his life direction. I will never know.

Morikawa and I, deep in Tosa, are searching for a bangai, an unnumbered temple we have found listed in old guidebooks. We have been told that it was abandoned for a time but that some years ago an energetic priest restored it.

With Temple Thirty-six behind us, we began this day by riding a ferry up a mountain-rimmed inlet that thrusts miles deep into the coastline. There is a tradition, which we were happy to honor, that at this one place in the pilgrimage the Daishi granted henro permission to travel by boat. Landing we found a dirt road that took us first among flooded paddy fields, then through tangerine groves, now up the easy slopes of a forested mountain. We meet almost no cars and there is birdsong all about. The temple is said to be at the crest of the mountain, the Crest of the Souls of the Dead Who Have Attained Buddhahood. This is another of those mountains where the souls of the dead gather.

There is no mistaking the crest: the road falls away in both directions. We stand there beneath the trees. There is no sign of a temple. Then sighting a path that enters the woods, we follow it to a swift descent of steps hewn from the mountain.

It is not at all what I expected. I thought that we would find a small hermitage in the forest. We stand where a ravine ends against the mountain but from here the compound stretches wide and open toward a broad valley. The ground underfoot is raw gravel; the scarred walls of the mountain show where it came from. The utilitarian buildings have no patina of age. We move to the newest; it is the residence and we are ushered into the priest's study.

It is unusual for henro to come this way these days, he says as he welcomes us. He is a big, vigorous man, taller and huskier than I, open in his speech. Several times he is called to the entry to speak with people who have come to him, yet with us he is unhurried. I piece together his story.

"During the war in the Pacific I was in the navy medical corps. I served in Saigon and in a general hospital in Singapore. I came safely home because of my mother's prayers, because of her great faith in Kobo Daishi. Our home was beside the henro-path. She wanted to make the pilgrimage with me after the war, but she died just fifty days before I got home. The following year, at the age of thirty, I decided to become a priest. I wanted to pray for the peace of the dead, all the dead, Japanese and those we fought against.

"And I had worked beside doctors. I had learned that there are sicknesses that medicine cannot cure; only religion can help. Cancer—people suffering from cancer come here to pray for recovery.

"The university on Mount Koya offers an accelerated course for those like me who are called to the priesthood late in life. I went there to study. I learned about this place from a henro who had discovered it on his pilgrimage—small chapel in the forest, about to be destroyed. He urged me to save it. No one knew what had become of the former priest. During the war he had prophesied Japan's defeat, said it had been revealed to him that the nation would be scourged by fire; the secret police had taken him away and he was never heard of again.

"I searched the records back five generations to find the owner and I bought the land. Where we are sitting was a ravine sixty feet deep. To fill it in I cut away the mountain, leveled the land. I built a road, following the old henro-path, more than half a mile down the mountain so that cars could get up here. I myself felled the trees, hewed the timber, built these buildings. I have labored here twenty-four years trying to follow the example of the Daishi. Without faith I could not have done what I did.

"You know the legend that Kobo Daishi founded the Eighty-eight Sacred Places. I do not believe that, but he did wander all through Shikoku. It was a backward, primitive place: he built roads and bridges and irrigation ponds; he did social work among the people; he brought them a higher faith. He founded some temples and restored others. I have done what I've done to prove that the Daishi could do what he did."

As he has talked between goings and comings he has given us souvenirs, he has invited us to attend a goma fire ritual he will conduct presently, and he has told us we are welcome to spend the night here.

Returning after another talk with a caller he conducts us to the goma hall, the one building surviving from the temple's earlier existence. Speaking of the prayers he will offer he uses the word *ki'lo*: it indicates prayer powerfully reinforced by rites and mysteries, rites with an ancient flavor of exorcism, mysteries most often directed to cure sickness. It is beginning to dawn on me that this priest is a shaman.

Four women are kneeling before the altar; I wonder how long they have been waiting. We kneel a bit farther back. The priest checks the name, address, and age of each person present. The two women on our left are mother and daughter. He asks the mother how many children she has borne. He asks the daughter if she is menstruating; the way he puts the question flusters her. When she answers yes he rephrases his query; now she states that her period is finished (he must be guarding against ritual impurity). Satisfied, he asks her what year she was born: "The Year of the Snake." It is clear that she has come to be cured of some illness (from the conversation Morikawa thinks it is a throat condition).

The women on our right, though by their ages they could be mother and daughter, are not related. His questioning of them is less probing.

He announces that this will be a goma for the purpose of making our wishes come true. He turns to the altar and prays, naming each of us. For Morikawa and me he asks simply that our desires be granted and that we complete our pilgrimage safely.

A tower of sticks has been built. Intoning a litany, striking gongs and bells, he sets the fire. It flares high. He is silhouetted against flame. When the blaze begins to subside he rises and moves to the left of the altar. He summons the daughter. With his three-pronged ritual instrument—heavy with brass and symbolism he thumps her back and shoulders, then massages them forcefully. From a foot-high stack of tissues he grabs a few, moistens them with his mouth, holds them over the fire, and with those hot and smoky papers rubs her brusquely; throwing the tissues aside he seizes more; he rubs her hair and shoulders, her back and chest, her face and head. Once, the papers catch fire; he does not notice, rubs her head, and her hair flames. I start to cry out but he sees, beats out the flame. With hot papers he massages her neck, then grasping her head he snaps it to the right, to the left, forward and backward; each time we hear the crack of her spine. He seizes her by the thigh and the neck, picks her up bodily, thrusts her at arm's length face down over the fire; reversing his grip, he flips her over, face up. He sets her on her feet, kneads her again with his hands, thumps her with the three prongs of brass, propels her back among us.

I am mesmerized. It has been a violent, almost fearful performance— it would have been fearful but for his strength and his assurance.

He calls the mother. Her treatment is briefer and he does not hold her over the fire. I look to see which of the women on my right he will summon.

"America-san!"

Me? If I could speak—but no words come. I find myself rising, advancing to the altar. I am thumped, massaged, rubbed with hot and smoky papers. My neck is snapped, my spine cracked. And then, incredibly, he picks me up, holds me outstretched over the fire; the heat flares on my face. He reverses me; my back glows. I am again massaged and thumped. I float back to my place.

Morikawa is called. He does not get held over the fire.

The flames are burning low now. The priest sits again before the altar. The other two women are called in turn to kneel before him, receive a relatively perfunctory treatment. He is now ready to answer their questions.

The older woman is concerned about her grandson. He is twenty-three and has not yet found a wife; what should they do? Nothing, he answers; he will not find the right girl until he is twenty-six; she will come from the direction of such-and-such a village. Will he have more traffic accidents?—he has been involved in several. He cannot avoid such misfortune, she is told; he will have another and serious one in December.

The young woman's husband is giving her trouble. The priest listens, comments briefly, advises her that the man's name indicates he will never be a success as a farmer: he should change his occupation.

The priest rises. The women murmur their thanks, bow gratefully, and leave—I am certain they made an offering earlier. Others are already coming in to pray and to be counseled. We are again invited to stay the night. I have a feeling that we should, that I should talk more with this man. Morikawa points out that it is early afternoon and that we are expected at a temple in the next town. The priest does not press us. We set out.

My body is light, all soreness gone, but my thoughts are whirling. Is this priest exploiting superstition or do people need what he offers? I truly believe that faith can work miracles. I know that all religion has an element of magic. But how slippery is the line between seeking enlightenment in this world and seeking favors—the priest said "happiness." I wish we had stayed to talk longer with him, to explore the role in which he casts himself.

The road down the mountain is not as pretty as the road up. The hills are bare; road construction is in progress. One sight I will remember: a plot of clover between beds of rice seedlings, lavender bracketed by tender green.

The experience continues to haunt me. Occasionally, when we are talking with another priest I ask an opinion. One reply seems defensive: that kind of prayer has always been an element of Japanese Buddhism and of Shingon in particular, and after all, the bangai in the mountains has no members to support it; the implication seems to be that somehow the priest has to make a living. It is an answer that leaves me troubled.

A highly respected priest is unequivocal. "Proper priests of Shingon are not faith healers. When they perform goma they may feel that they receive a message but they do not divulge it. They keep it inside, and pray. Faith healing, telling fortunes—this is walking the back road."

The priest of a temple on a mountain that for ages has been a center for ascetic practice touches on the issue without my asking. "The spiritual descendants of the ancient holy men still come here to perform the religious exercises that they believe give them power. Some of these men and women are good people but some of them worry me—those who tell the fortunes of the gullible or try to cure illness by prayer. Sometimes the seriously ill depend on them: everyone hopes for a miracle. Priests must admonish such faith healers since they won't accept counsel from laymen."

As we near the end of our pilgrimage, the priest of the mountain bangai is still on my mind. I realize that we must talk with him again. Morikawa phones; he says that he will welcome us. We catch an early morning train for the four-hour trip across the island over its high spine of mountains. From the station we take a cab up into the hills to the temple.

The driver doesn't have to be told how to get there: he says he makes the trip often. Nor does he seem surprised to find four women sipping tea in the entry, waiting for a taxi in apparent confidence that one will be along soon. We get out; they get in.

The priest appears, as tall and sturdy as I remembered. He receives us warmly, asks about our pilgrimage, thanks us for coming so far to see him again. He talks of the holy men of Koya (as if he knows the reason we are here) and of the mystic power of the goma fire. "There are things that cannot be explained by science."

We are several times interrupted. When we were here before I thought perhaps he was busy because it was a Sunday and a day off for most people, but this is a weekday and there is a steady stream of visitors. Many of them he turns away because we are here; we ask him not to but he says they can come anytime and we cannot. He does receive a few: from his study we can hear the murmur of their worried voices and his confident one, and the sounds of shoulder thumping and spine cracking; they leave looking grateful.

He take us up the mountain, guides us into the forest along traces of the old henro-path a few yards from the road we walked forty days ago, points out gravestones along the path. On one we make out a date: the Month of the Boar, 1803. "There are twenty or thirty stones along this path but actually only a few graves are marked—those of pilgrims whose families were well-to-do, who could send money or come themselves to erect a stone. The poor and sick came to Shikoku hoping to die along the pilgrimage route and become part of its sacred soil. The bodies of most of them were just thrown down a mountainside or tossed into some ravine.

"About twenty years ago when I was digging to widen the road I heard a voice crying from the ground. Working very carefully, I unearthed a skeleton, a rice bowl, a pipe, and some old copper coins. I conducted a service and reburied the bones."

Back at the temple I ask what kinds of problems, what kinds of sicknesses, people bring to him.

"The kinds that can't be cured by medicine—stomach and intestinal disorders, neuroses, diseases that the doctors can't diagnose. The tensions of life today, the mental strains that we are subject to, combined with rich food and lack of exercise—these produce intestinal ulcers and all kinds of muscular pains. From neuroses to the athlete's foot we get when we put on shoes, modern life is hard on us."

He summons two women from the kitchen. "This woman was once a section chief in a telephone office. She had a breakdown and was put in a mental hospital. The doctors said she could never be released but I cured her four years ago.

"This other had an operation on her throat. They cut a nerve, destroyed it so that she was left with psychoneurosis. I cured her." The women second him. There is no questioning their sincerity. They work at the temple out of gratitude.

"You must not misunderstand. The Esoteric Buddhism of Shingon was not developed to cure disease but to achieve peace and a calm heart. We must know ourselves and see the interrelationships that bind us together and to the universe. Shingon is very profound, difficult to master. Most priests don't study hard. I undertook many spiritual exercises; I trained seriously. It is possible to see Buddha. I did once: I felt an ecstasy far greater than the climax of sexual intercourse.

"Now when I meet someone I can tell what kind of agony or disease possesses him. I know when someone is going to die soon or suffer a tragedy: I don't tell what I foresee but I try to implant the power to endure."

At last I ask the question I have crossed Shikoku to put to him: "You worked in a hospital during the war. You were a medical assistant. You have some knowledge of medicine. If someone comes to you with a disease that a doctor could help, do you recommend that he or she see a doctor—as well as offering your help through prayer?"

"I always ask first if they have been to a doctor. If they have not, I tell them to consult one. If it seems necessary I send them to a hospital at once." This is what I wanted to hear.

It is dark before we recross the mountains. Morikawa is dozing. I tell myself that this hard day has been worthwhile. My eyes close.

LOURDES

"It is better to say I'm suffering, than to say —
This landscape is ugly."

—Simone Weil

R emember my grandmother's small bottle of Lourdes water. A very cloudy glass Madonna. The precious liquid never seemed to be used, it just evaporated away. I remember her great length of rosary beads, also from Lourdes, that hung on the wall beside her bed. All her pieties had seemed strange, but endearing, because they were part of her, and her struggle, in her old age, towards some kind of atonement for a rather romantic past. Romantic anyway, as it was handed down to us. Her long affair with a Frenchman, when it ended, or maybe because she could not end it, she tried to take her life, by jumping from a window. She broke her hip, and always walked lopsided after that. Everything about her was at an angle; the wide-brimmed hat, the head, the mouth, the whole expression; all of it seemed to be a part of some sadness, a search for some forsaken self, that she seemed to find in her Catholicity. A Catholicity of rosaries, candles, blessings, novenas, and the greatest joy of all—her son. Born to her late, after her return to the original marriage bed. Her son became a priest; her most dreamed of, expiatory gift to God.

I left the train thinking vaguely of her, and the deep trench that her faith had been. Something gripping and sad; something dark, full of sorrow and longing.

Lourdes didn't seem like France. It was wet and cold. Heavy gray clouds over dark, green hills, hardly mountains. It felt like Ireland.

I wandered vaguely down the hill, riveted by all the brightly painted hotels. Madeleine, at Lisieux, had told me of a convent opposite the Grotto, but it was after 9 P.M. and the convent was a considerable distance from the station.

The bright hotels, that in Ireland might have read "Atlantic View" were here, instant reminders that you were in a place of pilgrimage. More pilgrims come to Lourdes than Rome or Jerusalem, over four-and-a-half million a year.

I wandered on past these eager hotel facades, all with "vacancies" in the window. Hotel Saint Therese, Saint Teresa, Saint Jude, Saint Antony, Saint Anselm, Pius 12th, Holy Nazareth, Angelus, etc., etc. There was even Hotel Solitude in the middle of it all.

Although it looked as if it might rain any minute, I didn't feel beckoned by any of the vacancies in the windows. Every so often something said "Grotto." I vaguely wondered if I should go there, but it was in the opposite direction to all the hotels.

The streets were completely deserted. Suddenly I heard footsteps behind me. A tiny, cheerful couple were coming very fast down the center of the road. They recognized me. I had asked them which platform for Lourdes, when we were racing for the train at Toulouse.

They were Roger and Josephine Arpin from the mountains of Saint Maurice. It was their holiday. Usually they went on holiday to relatives, but they had all died. They had been before to Lourdes. They told me to follow them to a very cheap lodging; many were very, very dear. Roger indicated the gleaming hotels all round us. They raced on, laughing and arguing with each other about the right direction to take. Two nuns looked extremely disapproving as we clattered past. At last, shrieks of joy, they had found it. La Familiale. A small hotel above a gift shop. Yes, there were rooms.

In the rain and gray cold, nothing seems more bleak than an empty gift shop, full of Marian pieties. A little girl was doing her homework in the shop. Encouraged by Monsieur, I bought the English guide. A fresh one, brought out after the Papal visit in 1983. Business was certainly not booming. In the little dining-room, Madame was working away at figures, on her typewriter. There was a party of school girls, that was all. Josephine and I had a *verveine* together. I also had soup and an apple. Roger had gone off to a bar. "He's a little like this," Josephine said, indicating with her elbow, frequent drinking, "but we manage." She was very amusing and direct, and quite convinced that there was no cheaper bed in the whole of Lourdes.

My room was four floors up, very small indeed, but with a large bed. The mattress was a dumpy mound of lumps and horsehair spikes and old brown feathers; as soft as cold porridge. There was a tiny square window looking out directly on to the Fort. I remembered that before the Marian Cult at Lourdes, this remote area of the Languedoc had had a fierce history; among other things the whole town was put to the sword by Simon de Montfort during the Albigensian Crusades.

I knew that the bed would play havoc with my back, but there was no space to think of putting the mattress on the floor. There was hardly space to stand. One night I thought, and Lourdes is a place for penance after all, not miracles. I had been told this so many times on my journey. The contemporary stress is on a place of reconciliation, prayer and recognition of the Cross; our part in the Cross.

The next day, my back made it abundantly clear to me that I must find fresh accommodation. I thought I should seek out the Convent of the Assumption first, and then return for the baggage, if I got offered a bed. I visited the *cachot*, that was nearby. The *cachot* was a disused prison lock-up that a cousin of Bernadette's family made available for the Soubrious when they were destitute. It was empty at the time, because it was felt to be unfit, even for prisoners.

You always have some preconceived ideas of a place, particularly anywhere as well known as Lourdes. People often mention the horrors of the gift shops; all the tasteless kitsch; the whole commercial bandwagon. I was expecting that, and real mountains. There is no drama about the landscape, there is typical, ash-white, spa stone, green hills and the racing river Gave.

The shape of the town and its relationship to the Grotto is laid out in such a way that you can easily visualize the walk, taken by the frail, asthmatic Bernadette from the *cachot* down to the area known as Massabielle, to collect firewood. It was here that the apparitions appeared to Bernadette, in 1858. It is quite some distance down the hill, past the fort, to the river, and then on to what must have been a wild, wooded area. High, under heavy, grey-black, overhanging rocks, is the Grotto, only a little way back from the river. The Gave is a wide, fast-moving, dash and swirl of greenish water.

Just as at Rocamadour, it is perfectly possible to go from station to Grotto without passing the gift shops, and the general trading buzz. The vast basilicas, both above and below the ground, the baths and grotto, the hospitals and Way of the Cross, they are all in the enclosed domain of the Grotto, separate from the other town. In fact I felt sorry for the traders, they get continual flack from journalists, but obviously what they sell is what the pilgrims want, and buy, again and again. It all seems like a very legitimate market force. Certainly the objects are fairly mind-blowing, but not all the innovations seem to catch on. A life-size, moving crib, was continually empty; the nodding donkey outside, to the strains of Corelli, seemed no incentive to entry.

That first morning, when I visited the *cachot*, it was fairly quiet, it was early in the day and not the peak season, there were few pilgrims. First, you go into a low-ceilinged room, which is full of photographs and memorabilia, then a Sister sorts people into small groups, ready to cross the narrow passage into the *cachot*, which is a single space, four by four-and-a-half yards. There is a very shallow, low, stone sink and beside it the chimney breast, with an open grate. There are two shuttered windows. The slate window sills are deep enough to sit on. The atmosphere is gray and still. People simply come in, and stand and stare in silence. It is hard to imagine that a family of six ever lived here. They had two beds and a table. The windows could never be opened to let out the smoke from the fire, as the flies and smells from the yard outside would have been intolerable. It must have been terrible to wash clothes, and cooking pots, and bodies, just in that small sink. I sat for some while on the window sill beside the sink. Maybe Bernadette and the family had sat there, or possibly, it had housed pots and pans and plates. How damp and dark it must have been. Living in such terrible, brutalizing conditions, faith would be forced, either to become dead and bitter, or heroic. The usually vague, comfortable, middle ground, would seem impossible. If you believed in God, and His Love, and His Mother, with her love, you might very well think of little else. It would be the only imaginative thread to lead you, to some extent, away from a living hell.

In that little room, it was impossible not to feel close to the young girl, with the dark, serious, heavy-lidded eyes, the full mouth and the round face, framed by a headscarf; the shawl, and the gathered peasant skirts. Bernadette had severe asthma, she was always unwell after her recovery from cholera. That walk down to the grotto for the fire-wood must have been exhausting for her.

Bernadette, the simplicity and dire poverty of her short, dramatic, public life, subsequent to the eighteen apparitions, feels real and close to you in the *cachot*. Finally "Aquero," That One, which is how Bernadette referred to the Madonna, gave her name, after insistent requests from Bernadette, encouraged by the parish priest.

I am the Immaculate Conception.

From that moment, the parish priest, Father Peyramale, was convinced that the visions were authentic. Consistently Bernadette remained firm and calm against intolerant and aggressive handling. She insisted that there were no miracles as far as she knew. Lourdes was not about miracles. The lady had said to build a chapel above the grotto, and to pray, especially for priests, and to process. The lady had simply indicated to Bernadette where the spring was, and said she could wash her face there. Clean water would have meant far more to Bernadette, living in the *cachot*, than we can imagine.

There were many other springs and Marian shrines in the area. Lourdes might have remained simply a chapel by a river, with local pilgrims coming to the place. In 1862 the Bishop of Tarbes authorized the cult. Huge crowds came. The professionals, the Garaison Fathers, moved in. They were expert organizers of visionary moments and subsequent pilgrimage. The *domaine*, the land surrounding the grotto, was bought. The train came.

The Catholic Church, particularly in France, was consistently threatened during these times. In 1870 the Dogma of Papal Infallibility was defined. In 1871, during the Paris Commune, the Archbishop of Paris was murdered. Catholics needed to show strength and solidarity. In 1872 there was a pilgrimage of twenty thousand to Lourdes, predominantly of Royalists. There seems to have been more to the founding of Lourdes than Bernadette, her visions, and the fairly low key demands of Our Lady, for a chapel, prayers and processing.

I made my way up on the outer edge of the town, to the Convent of the Assumption, which is a substantial building, standing alone in its own considerable, high grounds. The back of the convent looks out across to the Grotto, the river, hills and woods, and the vast area of green grass, where pilgrims picnic and pray. All through the day small groups celebrate mass, up and down the banks of this belting pulse of green water.

The convent had been a school, now, like so many of these religious houses, it is a retreat house. It accommodates both large, organized retreats, and small, personal pauses, for those known to the Community.

The Sister in charge registered some surprise that I had not written in advance. Prudence again, or rather a lack of it. Although I feel inclined to believe in the alternative prudence, of letting things happen. At first the Sister found definitely, no bed; no space whatsoever. Then after another look, good heavens yes, a cancellation. There was a bed after all. The Sister escorted me upstairs and showed me into a room, with its own douche and lavatory. In the room was a small writing table. The bed itself was marvelously hard. It was certainly the highest standard of accommodation, comfort and privacy I had experienced.

There were about fifty Sisters from various Orders from all over the world, staying in the convent for a week's retreat. They were from Canada, South America, the Philippines, and various parts of Africa, also France itself. I would eat with the Sisters in silence. Three meals a day; please attend all meals. There was a rota for washing up, laying of tables, clearing etc. There was not only a key for the room, there was a series of keys available, to open the gates on the private route, under the railway and into the *domaine*, the area of the Grotto, basilicas etc. There were two libraries in the convent and one small salon, with a balcony, looking directly across to the Grotto. The price, including all three meals, was less than La Familiale. Roger and Josephine would be amazed.

I felt very grateful to Madeleine's advice. The convent was extremely bright and cheerful, the Sisters were young and active, full of humour, and very hardworking, between the regular hours of Sung Office in the Chapel.

But there was something about Lourdes itself, which made me feel deeply apprehensive. From the small salon I saw the Grotto just as I had seen it before on so many postcards, all my life. There were the flickering candles and the steady, slow stream of people. I must admit, I felt nothing but dread at the idea of going down there. I don't know why, but there seemed to be this cold, grey dark over it all, despite the vast, white statues; that kind of harsh, screaming white, that is almost as bad as chalk slipping on a blackboard.

Again and again I made my way down, and up, and down again. I was perplexed and miserable at my own chilling dismay and deep unease. All day there were people waiting outside the baths, waiting to be admitted through the blue and white curtains; many more women than men. All day there were bustling crowds at the brass taps, filling plastic water containers, bottles, and glass madonnas, and washing their faces and hands, and drinking. It is very clear water. It has the cold sting of stone in it. I washed my face, and drank from my hands when there was a free tap. All day, groups from all over the world, bearing banners of their town, parish, country, or Organization, gather for mass by the river, or to make the steep Way of the Cross, up the wooded hill above the Grotto. There are long queues for candles, huge candles, that are never able to burn themselves out, until February, when a giant fire cleans up all the long, left-over lengths of wax.

Every afternoon there is the Procession of the Blessed Sacrament. The sick who are able to walk, gather under the trees on metal benches, which have *malades* written on them in blue and white enamel. The place in front of the Basilica of the Rosary is contained by a great swoop of steeply rising, balustrated walkways that run up to either side of the door to the Basilica of the Immaculate Conception. Every afternoon the balustrades are packed with people watching the progress of the procession.

The procession moves out from the Grotto itself. The *brancardiers*, the officials of Lourdes, keep the crowds in check. The procession always takes the same route, from the Grotto, down the esplanade, and upwards towards the basilica. On past yet another crowned Virgin, into the area directly in front of the church, where the sick are waiting in wheelchairs, and on stretchers, or in the rather wonderful, rickshaw-like vehicles, with their bright blue hoods, a protection against sun or wind or rain. They are pulled, rather than pushed. Every day, before the procession is due to start, you are suddenly aware of a flurry of activity as nurses, nuns and *brancardiers* race their rickshaws to get the sick into position.

Different pilgrimages head the procession each day. The shape and feel of the procession alters with each pilgrimage. There are always the priests leading, and then the canopy and the Blessed Sacrament held high in its star of gold. Once the processing is over, the priests walk slowly among the sick. Again and again the blessed sacrament is raised in blessing over them. This is sometimes the time of miracles. Certainly there have been many miracles and dramatic remissions of chronic disease, sometimes at Lourdes, sometimes months or years after a visit. Authenticating miracles is a fairly grisly business. Miracles are not emphasized now. People say: I'm not here for a miracle; just for hope, peace, and reconciliation. But when you see crumpled little people in pushchairs and lying on the stretchers; distorted limbs, lost, stiff expressions, the concept of cure must be somewhere in the mind of the brave and loving parents and carers. The majority of the sick do seem to be old, and to be women; rows and rows and rows, tucked in by brightly-knitted nursery blankets, a mosaic of colored squares. From dawn to dusk the *domaine* is a buzz of movement and activity.

In front of the Grotto itself, there is a large area of smooth stone; it is sometimes closed, sometimes open, depending on the time of day. Always a steady stream of people move slowly round the Grotto, below the dark niche in the rock, where the tall, white statue stands. Bernadette, when shown the statue exclaimed, "My God, how you deface her." She was also shown an icon of the Madonna, and was said to have felt "Aquero" was more like that. But her reactions were virtually disregarded, the blue sash is there, as Bernadette said, and the rosary beads, and the clasped hands, and the eyes lifted to Heaven.

The extraordinary force of simple, accumulated pressure is brought home to you, by the marble-smooth surface of the gray rock, where every day, for over a hundred years, hands have felt their way as they go towards the spring, now covered under glass, and out once more into the light.

In the evening there is the Candlelit Procession. It takes the same route as the Blessed Sacrament Procession. Everyone carries a lighted candle. The hymns, the Credo, the Salve Regina and of course the Lourdes Hymn itself, sound out clearly above the crowd from a loudspeaker system, but it seems to lessen rather than encourage the voices of the pilgrims. Intermittently there are warnings given against crime. Thieving is a major problem.

The Basilica of the Rosary, and above it, the Basilica of the Immaculate Conception, are nineteenth-century gothic. High, pointed towers rise up against the hills. The buildings are constituted in a gray-white cold stone. Accommodating spaces for vast crowds never cease to be built. There is a new Sanctuary of Lourdes, inaugurated as recently as 1988. It has a rather somber South Bank feel to it. It can accommodate five thousand. It is used for conferences as well as worship. The main Sunday masses are usually co-celebrated underground in the Basilica of St Pius 10th, inaugurated in 1958. This basilica has a capacity for twenty-five thousand. It is rather like being in the rib cage of a whale.

There are other chapels, the Chapel of Reconciliation, a little room with wooden cubicles on every side. Robed priests wait with their breviaries open. Above the cubicles is written the language within which confession may be heard. Margery Kempe would have been delighted, her non-existent access to foreign tongues made the sacrament of penance in faraway places like Rome, Jerusalem, and Compostela a considerable trial for her. It often gave rise to more scruples than a sense of forgiveness.

There are Foyers of the Missions, Pavilions of Vocation and many cinemas, with non-stop films on Bernadette and Padre Pio. And of course there are the shops and cafes, with easy ramps for wheelchairs.

For me, the *domaine* was a grippingly sad, gray, somehow static place. Thousands and thousands of people, all with inward looking eyes, as they stare out. I felt nothing but increasing alienation and dread. I have many friends who have been greatly helped by visits to Lourdes, both as the sick, and as parents of the sick, and as helpers of the sick. Thinking of their joy and comfort with the experience only made me more perplexed and anxious, with my own dark, miserable, utterly dejected sense.

Of course, as I processed and wandered generally about, I had to wonder where my feelings were rooted. Why did it seem so to me? Was it
muddled belief?

There is a strong mix in Lourdes of papal preoccupation and the dog-
matic edge of the Immaculate Conception. For me, the whole Madonna
bit can be difficult, because the inconography, almost all the images have
been made in the language of a male view of female purity. Maybe for
women, their view of purity might be of strength; real form. Something
wise and known; way beyond girl. That kind of female expression is hard
to find. I can cope much better with mysterious, little black stubs of
Madonnas, as at Le Puy or Rocamadour, they seem like coals of fire grown
cold, but they still remain alive with energy and mystery.

The need to define Papal Infallibility as late as 1870 has always seemed
to me to demonstrate a lack of faith in the gifts and power of the Holy
Spirit to mankind. The message of Christ is so huge, so clear, perfectly
understandable by anyone. Love God. Love your neighbor. Love your
enemies. It seems enough to be going on with. Who needs dogma?
Continued emphasis on papal authority seems to infer this lack of faith. It
seems to put Pope before the Holy Spirit as guardian of the Church.

In his book *The Marriage of East and West Bede,* Griffiths writes: "The
fact that Rome became the center of Christendom is an accident of history, and the Bishop of Rome only acquired his present position after
many centuries. One may hold that this development was providential,
but there is no reason to believe that the present structure of the papacy is
permanent, or that the Church may not acquire a new structure in the
context of future history."

Even though it may not always seem so, history, like the river Gave
moves fast and furiously.

Perhaps it was the nineteenth-century religious art that so depressed
my spirits. Without the disciplines that are imposed on icon painters and
Buddhist artists, it is easy for sacred images to become increasingly deca-
dent. Without some sense of abstract awe, images easily deteriorate into
extremely sentimental human terms.

I heard many complaints that times had changed. No one made the Way of the Cross on their knees. The *brancardiers* talked to one another as they wheeled the sick, once they would have been saying the rosary. There was less silence. People even spoke in front of the Grotto. People even picnicked by the river. "Everyone now is egoist," one local lady said. I'm still not sure what she meant to imply.

It got colder and colder. I found the walk up and down the hill from the convent quite a task. Most of the nuns on retreat buzzed up and down, taking in two processions each day. I felt ridiculously wretched. Perhaps I had just run out of steam. In the convent grounds, against a far wall, beyond rubble and overgrown grass, there were thirty red-brick, disused rabbit hutches. Each one had an arched wooden door, under a curve of bricks. They were beautifully made, stepped in tiers, to follow the sloping shape of the ground. I began to find them and the river, the two most sustaining sights.

Life at the Convent of the Assumption was a comfort. There was something very earthing about those silent, five-course meals. They were always so carefully presented; the napkins rolled carefully and put back afterwards in the numbered cubby holes. There were generous supplies of red wine. Throughout the meals taped music was played. Vivaldi, Beethoven, a minuet, a pavane. The tables were hexagonal. In silence, character comes strongly to the fore. The diffident, the humorous, the disapproving. I became fascinated by the physical resemblances. The feel of the skin, and the thin, almost vanished lips. The watchful, rather wistful eyes; a kind of attending wisdom. Many were small, rather homely figures, but full of energy. They reminded me of old-fashioned nannies, as in *Brideshead Revisited*. Nannies that might be found knitting in the upper rooms of a large house. Nannies, who know so much of what goes on, but say so little, unless asked. The glance, the pause; a language of nuance and inference, while folding clothes or stirring tea. While ecclesiastical dramas run on in the grand rooms and curia corridors, maybe these simple "nannies" keep the fire going; mending and stitching, giving comfort and consolation. They are certainly a strong force always to be relied upon.

One evening three Sisters approached me. I was, they realised, a Little Sister of Saint Charles de Foucauld, might they speak with me, they had friends in the Order. I couldn't believe it. A second time. I had to ask what had given them the idea. They became very shy, and then blushing they told me . . . "Well . . . the little Sisters wear blue . . . and their clothes are often very worn and shabby . . ." This must have been my rather long and faded Hobbs skirt, a cast-off from my daughter. It had gained a certain patina of the road, and had become increasingly comforting to me because of that.

There was a diverting small group of people staying in the convent, not nuns, and not on retreat. Tell us about Margaret, they asked eagerly one morning. Well, I have never voted for her, I began. No. No. not that Margaret, they interrupted. Margaret. Margaret, your Princess. They were eager for news. One young woman was keen to put me in touch with Charismatics in Kent. Denise spoke in tongues. She explained to me that whereas Lucifer can understand prayer, he realizes that the Our Father, or Hail Mary are addressed to heaven, tongues on the other hand are safe from him. They are a direct, coded route to the Almighty.

As the gray days passed I wondered about the baths. There were always long queues. Some of the nuns were bath addicts, some had never been. All stressed that the point was penance. It was an act of faith.

One morning there was a blustering north wind between heavy showers. The *domaine* was practically deserted. No one was queueing for the baths. I paused by the sign. I was promptly ushered in through the blue and white curtains. There was the sound of piped music. More blue and white curtains and then into the waiting cubicle, which takes six bodies at a time. A pilgrimage from Kildare was bathing, so the helpers were all speaking English. There were one or two strays, not from the pilgrimage. I was assumed to be a stray. "Dutch or German most probably, she can't understand a thing," I heard one of them say of me. "Petticoat and bra on," they yelled, "everything else off."Dazed women peeled down their clothes. One elderly woman was busy unwinding bandages from a raw, superating wound. But you could hardly look, speed was the thing. Another curtain, and there was the bath, like a narrow, stone cattle trough, just a step down. Utterly paralyzed, and very grateful to be assumed to be Dutch, I stared for a second into the clear water. Then the ladies, one at each side, with horrifying speed, yanked off the bra and petticoat, and threw a large, wet length of mutton cloth over the body, presumably in the interests of some kind of modesty.

"In now, sit down, sit down, not your head." I suppose for speed they pushed on the shoulders. I felt as if I had gone through some fairground curtain, into a ghost train, where things flapped at you, and voices called. One of the women grabbed up a small, white statue from the end of the bath. "Kiss our lady and say your prayer . . . now." The statue was put to my lips. It was all over in seconds. A dunking. Mutton cloth off. Clothes on. No towels.

Seconds later, I was beside that marvelous, loud, pounding river. There was a curiously warm feel on my wet body. Water and stone once again. A place of water and stone. For me, some sort of atrophied sadness; something frozen in time; something beyond any coherence I could tap into.

The last day was glorious, with a really warm sun. I met many English people at the cafe tables. Pilgrims from Catford, Croydon, and Carnarvon. All were thrilled with Lourdes. For most of them, it was a longed-for visit. "She'll get you back if you ask her, she'll always find a way," one man said from his wheel chair. They talked of peace of mind and spiritual healing. Rita, one of the helpers, described how suddenly, many years ago she had decided to take a child suffering from Down's syndrome to Lourdes. She had cashed in all the family savings. Her husband had been furious. But from that beginning, they now had a regular business, taking the sick to Lourdes. They had a special ambulance vehicle, with a lift for wheel-chairs. Rita said that the benefit for those isolated by disease and disability was incalculable. Suddenly on the pilgrimage, in a group, they were wanted and loved. They were the priority. It was often hard for them when they had to return home.

In Rita's party, there was a very charming Yorkshire man—Bill Alexander. He was over eighty. He had been to Lourdes four times. I asked him what Our Lady meant to him? He was eager to reply.

"She's the love of my life, Jini. It's like this. In the war we'd have photographs, wouldn't we, the wife and kids. And we'd look at them, and feel close to them. That's how it is with Mary. I have her there, at home, up on the piano. I took up the piano when my wife died. A bit of Beethoven. A bit of Scott Joplin. I'll turn to her when I'm playing . . . What do you think, Mother? How is it? It's all right lad . . . Carry on, carry on. Lourdes is sad. Of course it's sad, but it's wonderful. I'll tell you this, Jini, if they don't feel it when they come, then there's something wrong with them."

I was glad Bill felt so certain and so happy. I was glad also, that I had my ticket for Spain, booked to Irun for the next morning. From there, as soon as I could, I would make my way to the far west of Galicia. To Santiago de Compostela.

GARY   PAUL   NABHAN

LA VERNA'S WOUNDS

From Montane Sanctuary to Chestnut Grove

Monte La Verna was where we would start our sauntering in earnest, after a good night's sleep in a chalet-style lodge. Our third-story rooms, although without heat, were far more comfortable than the Sasso Spicco cave on the mountain that Francis first visited in 1213 and to which he would return for retreats five more times during the course of his life. This was where Francis spent forty days fasting in the fall of 1224. While he prayed outside his cave on the night of September 14 of that year, the flesh of his hands and chest began to open and ooze with wounds, and he received a vision of being lanced and nailed to a cross. Villagers of nearby Chiusi della Verna still tell of what their ancestors saw that night: the summit of Monte La Verna was illuminated by an unearthly light, but no one immediately knew its origin. It was not until much later, when the companions of Francis saw his Christlike wounds, still oozing with the suffering of the crucifixion, that they guessed that the stigmata had been given to him that evening.

The mountain was not illuminated but shrouded in fog when Ginger and I arrived at the hillside village of Chiusi della Verna. We heard a chorus of mountain singing like that which Francis may have heard when he first ascended the peak with his brothers Masseo, Angelo, and Leo in 1213. As we began to climb the narrow trail up to La Verna's summit, I recalled the story of the songbirds that had welcomed Francis:

> When they were come nigh at the foot of the very rock of La Verna, it pleased Saint Francis to rest a while under an oak tree that stood by the way, and there standeth to this day; and resting beneath it Saint Francis began to consider the lay of the place and of the country round about. And lo, while he was thus pondering there came a great multitude of birds from divers parts that, with singing and fluttering of their wings, showed forth great joy and gladness, and surrounded Saint Francis, in such wise that some settled on his head, some on his shoulders, and some on his arms, some on his bosom, and some around his feet. His companions, beholding this, marveled greatly, and Saint Francis rejoiced in spirit, and spake thus: "I do believe, dearest brothers, that it is pleasing to our Lord Jesus Christ that we abide on this solitary mountain, since our sisters and brothers the birds show forth such great joy at our coming."

The birds welcomed us, but so did birdshot in the distance. It was hunting season, and the sound of gunfire would stay with us throughout our trip, up until we celebrated the Feast of Saint Francis in Assisi. For the moment, however, no hunters were in sight, for the La Verna forest itself is a national monument where hunting is prohibited.

"Now I feel like we've begun," Ginger said as we climbed toward La Penna, the 3,800-foot precipice at the summit of La Verna. I could not answer her; I was panting and scanning the forest as we walked.

We climbed the ancient cobblestone path up through the oak, beech, and fir, rose hips, brambles, and ferns. The trail was an old one; in places, the cobbles had been buried by sediments moving down from open, eroded areas. In more protected spots, moss completely covered the limestones, the fence posts, and the trail markers. It was difficult to walk the trail without imagining Francis on the very same route. I spotted a white-haired, bent-over man, seated on a bench not far from the trailhead.

"Pardon me, but how far is it to La Penna?" I asked.

"Walking vigorously, fifteen minutes to the sanctuary and another fifteen to La Penna. Not so bad, eh? There is a paved road to the chapels and lodging where his cave was at the sanctuary, but you can stay on this little trail all the way up."

As the fog became thicker, we passed lichen-covered wooden crosses, shrines, and little stone chapels. Then, suddenly, we were vaulted off the forest pathway and into a huge parking lot serving no less than fifteen buildings crouched around the original chapel of Santa Maria degli Angeli. Some of the buildings were multistoried and enormous. I began to realize that my expectations had been naive, particularly the one that the little hovels and caverns that Francis had loved would have been kept free from Catholic monument building. It did not matter to most visitors that Francis had lived according to the Gospel's guidelines for transients and faunal migrants: "Foxes have their holes and birds have their roosts, but the Son of Man has nowhere to lay his head." Francis himself had taken a dim view of the followers who had not even waited for him to pass before they began to erect monuments to him and to their cause, taking over universities and grand monasteries. The La Verna hermitage I could see was part of the same syndrome.

This complex of chapels, living quarters, and galleries was wondrous in scale and splendor. La Verna focused not only on Francis but also on other early Franciscans who were later granted sainthood; Bonaventure and Anthony now had their own separate chapels. The whole place was worked up in stately gray stone, embellished with Delia Robbia terracotta. And it was all too much to behold; I failed to make it past all the murals depicting the life of the saint, for the corridor that they lined was as long and as intimidating as any I had ever walked.

Instead, in less than half an hour, I succumbed to something akin to claustrophobia—or was it a fear of too much sheen? All the rough edges of

Francesco's life seemed worn smooth and shiny by so many people passing by and polishing his image. I longed to sense the dark, difficult, unembellished parts.

In that corridor, I could only see how Francesco and his poor brothers, among the first to take vows of voluntary simplicity, had been turned into celebrities and how their hovel-like chapels had become more like theaters or wax museums. Saturated, I impulsively walked up to the first door I saw and opened it, hoping to find a way out, perhaps a stairwell back to the trail. But that is not what I found.

There in front of me was a moss-covered grotto, luminous with the diffuse daylight that had filtered through the fog and rustling with a breeze that shook all the leaves in the trees above it. I did a double take: had I just entered an atrium? No, it was simply a room with no walls other than the Mountainside, no ceiling other than the canopies of beeches, and no floor except the moss and decaying leaves.

"If Francesco were alive today, he would make this his quarters," I chuckled to myself. Then, another double take: when I had turned in a semicircle to scan the entire grotto, something caught my eye. Steps led down to a cave with a small sign beside its opening: "Letto de San Francesco." These *were* his quarters, the Sasso Spicco, his refuge during forty-day fasts and his inner sanctum where he finally faced his fears, doubts, and vagrant dreams.

I slipped behind a fence meant to keep visitors from banging their heads or stubbing their toes in the darkness of the grotto's fissures. I stepped down a few stairs into the shadows of the cave. There, I wedged myself between two rocks like a lizard, and let my pores absorb as much of that space—cold, dark, and musky—as they could. Regardless of the hour of the day, regardless of the fog, regardless even of the trees and the rock itself, the grotto's innermost space was not without light.

I remembered the words of Susan Saint Sing, who felt that it was no coincidence that Francesco had finally made peace with the world while nestled within the darkness of the earth: "Francis found something in his cave, something so profound and startling that his whole life was changed. . . . It was as tangible as a solid wall, yet at the same time as elusive as the fog. It kept his heart waiting. Then one day, it stayed and never left again."

This grotto was a cove at the edge of a sea of night fog. I came out of it with a sense of relief that the rustic cave of poor Francesco had not yet been buried beneath a gilded basilica. It was still possible to remember here, as Franciscan Murray Bodo wrote, that Francis sought out "lonely places." Why? "To burrow into the earth in search of a treasure which lies hidden from those who live only on the surface." Perhaps I too was walking a lonesome highway to seek out such hollows; the hollowness that I felt inside after my divorce needed to be met in its darkest depths, not painted over on the surface to make everything look fine.

I found Ginger, and we walked up the trail past the walled enclosure of the hermitage, following a ridge that would, on most days, have provided an overview of the surrounding valleys and mountains. Today, because it was fogged in, it gave us no better sense of where we would be going. "That's okay," said Ginger, flashing one of her large, lovely smiles that would continue to endear her to me over the course of our pilgrimage to ether. "The way will reveal itself," she said, partly in parody of the conversation we had had the day before but mostly in true enthusiasm for whatever came along.

As we ascended through the mists above the hermitage and groped our way along La Spina della Verna, we began to notice one floral signpost after another assuring us that we were on the right trail. Wherever the brown-robed brothers had erected shrines, statues, or stations of the cross, someone had recently come along and placed in their midst small bouquets of cyclamen—or *panporcino,* as cyclamen is called here. It is a carmine-colored primrose whose twisted petals unfurl as they open, like an umbrella. Also as they open, they release a perfume that pervades the air around for them for several yards. I loved the way these hardy little plants offered such color and fragrance to an otherwise muted world. They would show up again later on our pilgrimage, and again they would be in a special place.

Soon we had climbed to the top of La Verna's forest, where we could encounter beech, fir, ash, and oak of enormous girths. Always a tree hugger, even I was overwhelmed here: I gave one of these giants four consecutive embraces as I moved around its circumference, and I still had not come full circle. Forest historian J. V. Thirgood has seen this phenomenon of large relictual trees elsewhere in forests long associated with saints: "The marked difference in the plant cover of sacred ground—cemeteries, shrines, and marabouts—[as opposed to] adjacent profane ground, may be seen in most Mediterranean countries. . . . In such protected situations, there are differences in the composition and density of plant formations, and in the height and girth of trees."

I had hoped that such dignified trees would still be standing at LaVerna, although I knew that most of the Tuscan forests had not fared well over the last six centuries. In 1849, Giuseppe del Noce compared Tuscan records of fifteenth-century forests with similar records newly placed in his hands. Over those four and a half centuries, most of the major tree species in Tuscany had seen their numbers reduced by 20 percent.

Yet in just the century and a half since Giuseppe del Noce's reckoning, an equal number of trees have been lost from the Tuscan countryside, for fields and pastures have been mechanically cleared on hills earlier thought to have been too soil-poor and precipitous to serve farmers and herders. Other wooded mountainsides have remained too difficult to work, but even so, no more than 60 percent of the forests that were known in Tuscany during the days of Francis persist today.

Sacred groves like those at La Verna and those above Assisi on Subasio are reputedly among the last holdouts in this region. Such forest enclaves have been spared for spiritual rather than economic or ecological reasons. And they are highly esteemed precisely because they provide a clear contrast to the widespread deforestation around them.

On an earlier trip to Italy, I had mentioned to the World Wildlife Fund's Gianfranco Bologna that I was curious about the relictual plant diversity left on La Verna and Subasio. He had kindly cautioned me: "If you are expecting La Verna to be a good area of wildness, you will be disappointed. It is a good place for meditation, but it is not biologically rich any more like the Carceri forest on Monte Subasio . . . They are such small forests compared to what you might be used to in the Americas."

Ecologists like Bologna rightly recognize that the biological diversity of any forest is not merely related to how long a place has been preserved; it also reflects the size and habitat heterogeneity of the place. If similar forests are not too far away or if they are linked by corridors through which plants and animals can "migrate," diversity has a better chance of being sustained. La Verna may have included some of Tuscany's original vegetation, for it had never fallen beneath the plow. Nevertheless, the forest is hardly large enough or close enough to other kindred forests to retain much variety within and beneath its canopy.

I had hoped that the sacred mountains of Saint Francis would be refuges of biological diversity, but I could not tell for sure whether that was true here at La Verna. I would take up the same concern when I had more botanizing time on my hands at Monte Subasio, after Ginger and I had arrived in Assisi.

Now we began a blind descent from La Verna. Whether the Tiber valley were immediately below us or whether a mountain range rose between us and the valley, we had no way of knowing, for the landscape remained steeped in thick fog. We moved along as one does in pitch-black darkness, hoping to grab onto some tangible object and then feel our way forward.

Within the first half-mile, I made out a tree vaguely familiar to me, although it looked more like an upright shadow than a green, growing being. I eyed its large, saw-toothed, lance-shaped leaves. I might have seen it in some book before, but I was not certain that I had ever seen it growing in the ground.

"Ginger! Let's stop for a moment. I need to look this one up, even though its name seems on the tip of my tongue."

I unhitched the belts of my backpack and let its weight drop to my feet. I untied the top flap and rummaged through the pockets of the smaller knapsack inside where I was keeping a field guide to help me identify trees.

All the while, Ginger stood patiently with her pack still on, staring at the wet ground beneath her feet. Finally she asked, "Which tree are you trying to identify? This one with all the chestnuts underneath?"

I smiled, looking up at the tree, then down at the mound of nuts on the ground. I put the field guide away without even opening it. The European chestnut needed no more confirmation than its fruit.

While its identity was easy, I wasn't sure if it had been intentionally planted or had sprung up as part of the spontaneous roadside vegetation. That uncertainty, like others on this trip, would have taken an intimate knowledge of local history to resolve. I had no such knowledge, but I assumed that chestnuts had been moved around by humans for so long that their presence in this particular spot must reveal social as much as natural history. This chestnut had been a native to Europe prior to the arrival of human cultures but had disappeared from southern Europe during the Ice Age and taken refuge in southwest Asia. Prehistoric planters carried it out of eastern Turkey into Anatolia and Greece more than 3,500 years ago. They returned it to Italy, where it proliferated with the help of the human hand. Even those trees in Italian landscapes that look the wildest, even those in places unmanipulated by humans for decades, are among the most domesticated of all chestnuts in the Mediterranean region, for they did not arrive in Italy as wildlings but were fully domesticated by the time they were dispersed from eastern Turkey to the Apennines thousands of years ago.

As Ginger and I ambled onward, I noticed chestnuts tucked into every possible context: roadside hedges, dense forests of towering trees, orchard-like plantations of several acres, abandoned barnyards, and village plazas where no other trees were planted.

We continued on through drizzle and fog, coming across little traffic on the road except for herds of sheep being moved from one pasture to another. All the while, we were never too far from the silhouettes of that nut-bearing giant, *Castanea sativa.*

After our lunch at Caprese Michelangelo on the first day of walking, I saw a peasant farmer ducking into an open barn door after tending his fowl. He greeted us and seemed curious about travelers with backpacks, so I asked him about the chestnut.

"*Castagne.* We start harvesting in a little less than a month."

"Wood or nuts?"

"Nuts, for a sweet flour. Some people call it *farina di marrone.*" This term, I supposed, held an aroma of French culinary influence, wafting over the Alps and Apennines from the west.

"Do you harvest them from this forest?" I said, pointing to the patch of woods in front of us.

"From here, all the way up." He nodded his head toward the mix of dark greens, blue-greens, and yellows, somewhat obscured by fog, that extended all the way up to the mountaintop.

"Are the trees there very old?" I wondered aloud.

"Older than I can remember. Some of those trees, they say, are sprouts from trees planted centuries ago."

"The forest—it was planted by man?"

"Yes, of course. The *castagne,* it is one of our major cultivated crops. Look!"

The fog was lifting, as though a veil were rising, finally revealing the wooded face of the mountain above us. The entire mountainside was embellished with the shapes and colors of chestnuts.

I later learned that Italy produces more chestnuts than any country in the world and that I was walking through the heart of the central Italian stronghold for *Castagne.* The uplands between Arezzo, Tiburtino Alto, and Caprese Michelangelo form a sanctuary of one of the oldest tree-cropping traditions anywhere. A nut variety selected from the last locality—Michelangelo's birthplace—is the kind most frequently cultivated across eastern Umbria and western Tuscany. Nevertheless, the low frequency of cultivation of all chestnut varieties today can hardly compare with the constancy with which it was found in the country up until half a century ago, when over two million acres remained covered with chestnut canopies. Over lunch not long after the pilgrimage, Florentine scholar Antonio Cacopardo explained some of the complexity of chestnut forestry traditions to me.

"Keep this in mind: for hundreds of years, the chestnut in the Apennines was like wheat for the rural poor. It covered areas so extensive that it dominated the diet of mountain dwellers. It was their staple."

"Do people still rely on it as a mainstay?"

"No, and that's unfortunate." Antonio shook his head. "Modern Italy does not consume even a fifth of the nuts that were harvested historically."

"Is the decline due to the blight that damaged the trees several decades ago?" I wondered.

"The blight obviously had some effect, but the sad thing is that there was also a demise in traditional agroforestry skills that went hand in hand with the decline in the use of the chestnut as a food. Today, most of the chestnut stands are coming up in secondary growth [of other species], or else they are intensively coppiced for just one product. Before, they maintained chestnut stands of several different ages, each in its own way, to obtain different products."

Some three hundred chestnut products, I learned, ranged from the nuts themselves to tomato stakes, crossties, and fence posts through furniture and boat-building materials. Tannins were extracted from the bark and heartwood to cure heavy leathers. Shingles, panels, and musical instruments could be shaped out of larger logs run through planing mills. Antonio recited this litany of uses, sipped his drink, then continued:

"The two main ways of managing chestnut trees in the past were simply called *macchia* and *selva*. In *Macchia,* chestnut trees are kept short and coppiced for poles over a twelve-to-fifteen-year rotation. In *selva,* trees many decades old are tended for the nut harvest and selectively cut for furniture wood and long boards."

A few farming families tenaciously maintain the vestiges of this rotational scheme, a scheme that may take over a century to run its cycle. In Tuscany, one farmer we met was still very selective about which old trees he cuts from the *selva.* And in the gap opened by his harvest, he always plants more trees. Nonetheless, forestry for foodstuffs is now the exception rather than the rule in Italy, where more than half the remaining acreage is frequently coppiced for wood alone. The chestnut blight brought about a collapse in nut production, and by the time the trees had begun to recover, Italian tastes had shifted away from the *castagne* they had formerly adored.

The chestnut blight did not reach southern Europe as early as it did the United States, and the consequences were somewhat different in the Mediterranean than they were along the eastern seaboard. In the United States, the blight fungus may have been introduced with Japanese chestnut imports as early as the 1880s, but soon after killing all the old trees along the avenues of the Bronx Zoo, in New York, it moved rapidly to devastate wild forest and planted grove alike. In less than three decades, the fungus wiped out the equivalent of nine million acres of chestnuts within the eastern deciduous forests.

It became one of the world's greatest forest tragedies. As chestnut ecologist Sandra Anagnostakis wrote in its wake, "We lost a beautiful shade tree, tasty nuts, and exceptional lumber; wildlife lost its most dependable mast producer. . . . Sweeping away every mature American chestnut tree, the infamous blight cut through the New England hardwood forest like an evil plague." Though most wild trees are quite heterogeneous in their susceptibility to diseases, no American chestnut populations had ever been exposed to such a fungus, so virtually no genetic resistance had evolved. From Maine to Georgia, all attempts to protect native stands chemically or physically failed miserably.

Like the blight in the United States, the blight in southern Europe began with the inadvertent introduction of fungus-infected trees from Asia. Some say that around 1939, the blight began to spread around the Mediterranean from diseased nursery stock that had been transplanted into a northern Italian botanical garden; no one really knows its point of origin for sure. As in the United States, the fungus was dispersed both by sticky masses of spores that hitchhiked along with birds, insects, and small mammals and by another, dustlike spore mass carried by the wind. After the fungus entered a wound in the bark of a chestnut tree, it would grow to produce a canker that girdled the trunk. The old trunk usually died, but the base of the tree survived to produce new sprouts at the ground level. The tallest trees that I saw around Caprese Michelangelo were probably the first or second generation of sprouts that had emerged, then survived, following the first wave of dieback.

An oddity had occurred in Italy quite unlike anything noticed in America while the blight took its toll. In 1950, twelve years after the blight's appearance near Genoa, pathology professor Antonio Biraghi observed what he thought were resistant tree sprouts in the area of earliest infection. Even though the trees had been girdled, their cankers were healing, and the shoots rising from them expressed normal vegetative growth. Soon healing cankers and healthy growth were recognized in other areas of Italy as well, but only in areas where the disease had swept through twelve to fifteen years earlier.

As time passed, population after population was seen to recover. This puzzled Biraghi's colleagues, because true genetic resistance could not "spread" from one vegetative sucker to the next, nor could the blight fungus genetically lose its virulence overnight. Finally, Jene Grente, a French expert on fungi, found that there was something parasitizing the blight fungus in northern Italy. When he passed samples on to Sandra Anagnostakis working in New England, she found that Italian blight fungi were suffering from a viruslike infection. She got permission from the government and inoculated the blight fungus that was infesting the bark of American chestnuts. Once the Italian strains were inoculated on

American trees in a greenhouse, Anagnostakis demonstrated that expansion of the cankers was halted so that the trees could survive.

Throughout Italy, the viruslike infection spread on its own, and healing cankers formed as the fungus was nipped in the bud. The fungal disease could no longer penetrate as deeply into the bark, and the trees were able to produce healthy new wood. Forty years after the discovery of the blight in Italy, the disease ceased to be a major problem.

"Forty years!" I moaned to myself the first time I heard this story, stretching my soul up into the bark of the fungus-infected chestnut. "Will it take me forty years to overcome my sores? How long it takes us poor mortals to heal!"

By the time the chestnut groves began to recover, however, chestnut farmers had lost over 80 percent of their customary consumers. The only market remaining for chestnut flour—and it was rather small—was for pastry making. Antonio Cacopardo lamented this withering of a staple into a specialty, but he understood the economics at work: "Even today, chestnut flour is three times as expensive as wheat flour. It is used primarily for sweet pastries and confections. *Farina di marrone* has one disadvantage in the market today; for most modern consumers, it seems too sweet to eat in a meal with meat and vegetables or with beer. Unless you are accustomed to it, the farina tastes a bit too rich, too strong.

"But in the old days, they would make a fire, heat flat sandstone slabs, and put a chestnut leaf on top of each one after it became hot." Antonio put his hand palm up over his other hand, mimicking the placing of leaf on stone. "Then they would pour a liquid batter made from chestnut flour over the leaf, which would keep the batter from sticking to the stone. The result was an unleavened bread—a tortilla, really, like those you eat in Mexico. Yes, more like a thick tortilla, not bread in the typical sense."

"It sounds delicious," I sighed.

"Ah, but there is a problem with such foods nowadays. The trouble is, no matter how tasty and nutritious this *torta di castagne* is, the country people today are self-conscious about it. Eating chestnuts is a sign of poverty. Because wheat bread is eaten in the city, chestnut bread is associated with the poor country table. It is the same everywhere with native crops, no?"

I had been curious about the chestnut's taste and texture and about whether any country folk still used it for foods other than desserts. I also wanted to taste it myself. After Ginger and I arrived at Caprese, I took a side trip to the mountaintop village of Fagiollo, where I asked a woman working in her yard about the local availability of chestnut products.

"Would anyone have quantities of chestnut flour stored away? Is it common here?"

"Common? It's our life."

"Do many men here work the chestnut harvest?"

"Men? Do you mean grown men?" She mocked the walk of a stocky man swaggering. "It's not just men, it's all of us. We've been working the chestnuts since we were *bambini*.

"Well, then, where can I buy some chestnut flour?"

"Try the store up in town that has a sign for the local forest co-op."

The store was filled with local elders. Ginger stayed outside. I walked in, sticking out like a sore thumb.

"Farina di castagne?" The people in the store looked up at me, embarrassed by my question. The store owner read their body language, then politely replied, "Better to come back in three weeks, in November. The harvest hasn't happened yet!"

"Yes, I think I understand. But I won't be here then. I'm not from around here . . ." but as I tried to explain my situation, the old women in the store flashed me looks that emphatically stated that they already knew I was alien to their world. "I'll be far away by harvest time and unable to return for flour. Is there any left from last year's harvest?"

The locals looked up at the storekeeper for his response, then fidgeted with the goods on the shelves. He gave them an icy gaze, then turned back to me.

"I'm sorry, it's just not fresh. All we have left is old flour that has sat on the shelves for two or three months. These people think it loses its taste. Around here, I can't even give it away. "

The shopkeeper's father overheard the conversation from the next room and came in, smiling, thinking over the situation.

"If this young stranger wants some, let's give him some. He apparently doesn't know the difference. Try to find him a tightly sealed package in the back room. Make sure it's not stale. And give him some kind of discount, for God's sake. He doesn't seem to be a pastry maker, or he would know that he would need a fresh batch."

"Is that all it's used for? Just pastries?"

"No, no. You can make polenta, too."

"But do you make polenta—is it often made here?"

"Yes, here we do. Not everywhere, but here, yes."

I knew from my friends Beth and John Romer that chestnuts remain sporadically and seasonally used just to the south of us, on the border between Tuscany and Umbria closer to Lake Cortona. Ginger and I visited them there later. Just as John was pointing out to me the areas in their valley where their neighbor Orlando Cerotti still manages chestnuts on a long rotation, Orlando's wife, Silvana, walked down the lane carrying a basket filled to the brim with freshly picked foods. Silvana had been out harvesting enough green beans and lettuce to fill the basket, but on her way back from the garden, she had tucked wild amaranth greens and mint into her upturned apron. She looked like a walking greengrocer, comfortably moving down the lane in a rayon dress printed with flowers.

Silvana had learned to make sweet chestnut cakes from her mother, and she still makes them as her mother did a half-century ago. Beth Romer described Silvana's process of preparing *baldino di castagna* in the following way:

> The cake is made by mixing the soft sweet flour into a loose paste with water and some warm olive oil. When the paste is well mixed, Silvana pours it into a round, flat tin which has been oiled, again with olive oil. Sometimes Silvana flavors the cake by scattering rosemary over the top

and sometimes a little lemon peel cut into tiny splinters. To cook it she puts the flat tin on top of some embers beside the fire, then covers it with an old saucepan lid, on top of which she piles more hot embers. In this way she has constructed a primitive oven. This is how the cake was cooked when she was a girl, though now she very often puts it into her new oven on medium heat. The cake is done when the top has become a dark chestnut brown and has a cracked surface. There is also a delicious smell of nuts and chocolate. . . . The olive oil and the rosemary, so often the garnish for meats, impart a curious . . . old-fashioned taste.

As for the simpler, unleavened cake called *castagnaccia,* which once served as daily bread for many Tuscans, it has largely fallen out of use, Silvana and the Romers agreed. The reason? "It is a poor food that still brings back memories of deprivation."

The Cerottis and many of their neighbors continue to care deeply about what goes into their mouths and where those foods come from. Quite often, their other foods, like chestnuts, still come from the managed forests immediately around them. For that reason, it is a misnomer to call all this forest bounty a *wild harvest;* many of the trees that have been harvested were earlier planted, or pruned, or protected from competitors. Nevertheless, the hill people of Italy still consume many times the amount of forest products that the average American does—in fact, more than most forest dwelling Native Americans do today.

As Ginger and I walked down into the Tiber valley after our visit with the chestnuts and the Cerottis, she marveled at the beauty and the fine ecological tuning she sensed in their highly managed valley. "It's not wilderness, but it *is* a cultured landscape peopled at an appropriate scale," Ginger mused. I nodded in agreement, but glanced around, looking to see if it retained enough wildness to suit me. "Harmony!" Ginger added, slowing her walk as she noticed my intense interest in this landscape. "You're talking about people living *in harmony* with their surroundings, just as I've seen on the Hopi mesas or in the mountains of Nepal."

"Harmony, huh?" I said, chuckling.

"What are you grinning about, Gary?"

"Do you know what they called you back in the hotel in Florence, Ms. Harmon? *Signora Harmony.* The desk clerk kept referring to you as *Signora Harmony!* I think I'll call you *Sister* Harmony the rest of the trip. It fits you, and, yes, it fits this land."

As our shadows grew longer, bumping against one another, then merging with the coming darkness, Ginger and I walked on toward Anghiari. Long after the sun went down, we finally entered that hilltop town on the edge of the Tiber valley and began our search for an inn where we could gain some well-deserved rest.

———————— ▬ ————————

BRIAN BOULDREY is author of *The Genius of Desire* and editor of *Wrestling with the Angel, Writing Home,* and the *Best American Gay Fiction* series. He is associate editor of literature for the *San Francisco Bay Guardian*. His fiction and essays have appeared in *TriQuarterly, Harvard Review, Flesh and the Word, Sewanee Review, James White Review,* and *Zyzzyva*. His novel *Love, the Magician* is due spring of 2000 from Hayworth Press.

PICO IYER is the author of such books as *Video Night in Kathmandu, The Lady and the Monk, Cuba and the Night* (a novel) and, most recently, *The Global Soul.*

—

MARVIN BARRETT has been a member of the editorial staffs of *Time, Newsweek, Show, Atlas,* and *Parabola*. His fifteen books include *The Years Between* and *The End of the Party.* He is married to the writer Mary Ellin Barrett.

FELICIA CLARK's travel writing has appeared in Salon.com. She lives in San Francisco.

ANNE CUSHMAN is the author of *From Here to Nirvana: The Yoga Journal Guide to Spiritual India*. Her writing has appeared in the *New York Times,* the *San Francisco Chronicle,* Salon.com, and *Yoga Journal.*

GRETEL EHRLICH is the author of *The Solace of Open Spaces* and *A Match to the Heart: One Woman's Story of Being Struck by Lightning*. She lives near Santa Barbara, California.

RACHEL KADISH is the author of the novel *From a Sealed Room*; her short stories have appeared in *Prairie Schooner, Story,* and *The Pushcart Prize Anthology*. She lives near Boston and is at work on a book about Holocaust reparations.

SATISH KUMAR is the editor of *Resurgence* magazine and director of programs at Schumacher College. He lives in England.

JENNIFER LASH was the author of *The Burial* and four other novels. In 1986 she learned that she had cancer, and after a painful operation, embarked on a solitary pilgrimage through France. Throughout her illness she continued to write. She died in 1993.

ALANE SALIERNO MASON is an editor at W.W. Norton & Company. Her work has appeared in *The Norton Book of American Autobiography, Beyond the Godfather* (an anthology of Italian-American writing), *Vanity Fair,* and *Commonweal* magazine.

JOHN HANSON MITCHELL is the author of three books on natural history, and editor of *Sanctuary* magazine, published by the Massachusetts Audubon Society.

ABIGAIL SEYMOUR is a senior editor at US Airways *Attaché* magazine in Greensboro, North Carolina, where she lives with her husband, whom she met while walking on a local watershed trail.

OLIVER STATLER is the author of *Japanese Inn* and *Japanese Pilgrimages,* as well as *The Black Ship Scroll* and *Shimoda Story.* Since 1977 he has been associated with the University of Hawaii as an adjunct professor and a fellow in Asian Studies.

ALICE WALKER was born in Eatonton, Georgia, and lives in northern California. Her novel *The Color Purple* won an American Book Award and the Pulitzer Prize.

BARBARA WILSON's memoir, *Blue Windows: A Christian Science Childhood* was nominated for the PEN Center USA West's Creative Nonfiction Award and won a Lambda Literary Award for best lesbian autobiography. She is currently working on a travel narrative about the North Atlantic.

MICHAEL WOLFE is the author of *The Hajj: An American's Pilgrimage to Mecca* and *One Thousand Roads to Mecca: Ten Centuries of Travelers Writing about the Muslim Pilgrimage.* He lives in northern California.

MALCOLM X was born in Omaha, Nebraska, and after a checkered life, joined the Nation of Islam, an African American sect of Islam. After his pilgrimage to Mecca, described in this passage, Malcolm X embraced Sunni Islam and more orthodox standards of the religion. Biographers and followers usually refer to the "post-Mecca" Malcolm X when they talk about the man most efficacious in the fight for African American rights in the United States.